IMPACT!

Activities to Enhance Teaching & Learning

Carl Olson

65 Hands-on Activities that Make a Difference

Published by:

Educational Media Corporation®
P.O. Box 21311
Minneapolis, MN 55421-0311
(763) 781-0088 or (800) 966-3382
www.**educationalmedia**.com

ISBN 1-930572-41-7 or ISBN 978-1-930572-41-6
Library of Congress Control Number: 2005931029
Printing (Last Digit)
9   8   7   6   5   4   3   2

Production Editor—

Don L. Sorenson, Ph.D.

Graphic Design—

Earl Sorenson

Contents

Introduction 5
Dedication 8
Acknowledgments 9
About the Author 11
Part 1 • Energizers **13**
All Tied Up 14
Diversity Mixer 16
Hot Rod / Paddle Move .... (Impact Pak) 18
Rubber Band Jump 20
String Escape 21
Unlock Your Potential 23
Positive Energy .... (Impact Pak) 25
Brain Storming Ball .... (Impact Pak) 26
Focus Wheel 28
Giant Straw 30
Smile on a Stick 32
Air Bags .... (Impact Pak) 33
Are You Sound Minded? 36
Floating Cup Trick 40
Mouth Coil 41
Neck Breaker 43
Nose Breaker 44
Show'em Your Smarts 45
The More You Know the Better 47
Point of View 49
Expand Your Possibilities .... (Impact Pak) 51
Mind Power 53
550 55
Bounce Back 56
D'lite 58
Magic Archs 59
Reach Beyond 61
Short Circuit 62
Spring to Life 63
Three Ropes 64

The **Impact Pak** is available from:

www.energizerolson.com and
www.educationalmedia.com

Part 2 • Games **67**
Equal Distant Game 68
Mystic Writing 69
Ping Pong Ball Flick 73
Polar Bears Around the Ice Hole 75
Breaking Away 77
Surfer Wave Girl 80
When Someone Claps Twice 82
Captain is Coming 86
Banana Bandana? 89
Field Goal 90
King Frog 92
NFL Teams 94
Balloon Problem Solving Activity 97
Cup Stack 98
Part 3 • Initiatives **99**
Sticks 'N Stones .... (Impact Pak) 100
Who Spoiled the Fun? 104
Lighter Than Air 106
Snow Flake 108
Look Beyond 110
Pipeline 112
Sketch Book 114
Stress Relief 116
Build a Team 118
Candy X Candy Y 120
Can't Get It Back 124
Newspaper Fashion Show 126
Ownership 129
Shapes for Understanding 130
Keys to Understanding 133
Squat Game 135
Who Has the Power 140
Part 4 • Special Activities **141**
A Day In the Life 143
Family Numbers 144
Random Acts of Kindness 146
Leaving Your Mark 148
Resources **150**

The **Impact Pak** is available from:
www.energizerolson.com and
www.educationalmedia.com

Introduction

Good teaching that produces effective learning requires that teachers have knowledge of their subject matter. In addition, teachers must be able to present the material so it can be absorbed and practically applied. Learning is best achieved when the learner is able to understand the information and use it effectively. In her book, *Speak and Grow Rich,* Dotty Walters uses the following research statistics:

We learn and retain:

10% of what we hear,

15% of what we see,

20% of what we both hear and see,

40% of what we discuss,

80% of what we experience directly or practice and

90% of what we attempt to teach others.

Lecture or "chalk and talk" instruction often fails to produce effective learning. The experiential teaching methods advocated in this book, and in the workshops I conduct, do produce the learning needed for growth and maturity. Passively listening and not being involved with the information being presented is basically a left-brain activity. It is important to present the material to be taught in a meaningful manner. Experiential teaching follows a process in which activities relating to the subject matter are presented. This gives the learners practical application. The information is taken in by the left-brain while the creative right-brain is also stimulated. Learning theory states that 25% of people are auditory learners, 25% are visual

---

learned and 50% are tactical or hands on learners. Experiential activities tie these three types of thinking together for a more complete learning experience.

In the beginning, most education was done on an apprenticeship basis. People learned their necessary skills as they applied to the job they were being trained to do. Soon after the industrial revolution, child labor laws were established, requiring children to go to school. In the school setting, children were put into classrooms and teachers transmitted information as effectively as possible to their students. Good teachers have always worked in this model, but now they realize they must provide experiences to go along with the information being delivered. In addition to adding experiences to the learning process, it is important to process what has been learned. During this step a relationship is made between the material presented and the activity itself. Effective processing asks three basic questions:

1. **What?**
2. **So what?**
3. **Now what?**

In other words, **What** questions would simply relate to the activity being presented. Then, **So what** questions relate the activity to the information being taught. Lastly, **Now what** questions tie it all together so that understanding results. Processing should be part of good teaching. When the process has an experience as its basis, learning is more complete.

"The best learning is that which is self discovered."

—Carl Rogers

Experiential teaching makes this outcome happen. This type of teaching follows a five-step process. The diagram below shows the order and direction these steps should take.

Experiential Learning

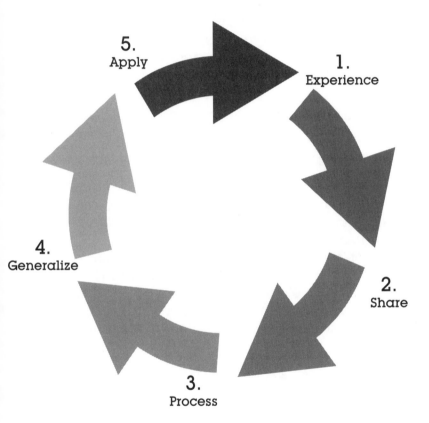

When setting up an activity, the teacher designs and sets up the experience. The main job is to make sure the directions are understood and the activity is safe. Next, the participants share the experience. The teacher allows this to happen and makes sure the directions are followed. Each group may experience the activity differently. A good teacher lets each group grow and learn at their own pace. In step three, the teacher gets to process and connect the activity to the desired learning. Lastly, the learning is generalized and applied to what is being taught.

An activity-centered approach to learning has additional benefits. The business world lists the following four qualities as desirable in their employees:

1. **Honesty**
2. **Teamwork**
3. **Communication skills**
4. **Good work ethic**

Honesty, teamwork, communication, and positive work ethic are direct results of experiential teaching. As I stated earlier, these concepts are not new. The direction teachers go with their active learning instruction is only limited by their creativity. The by-products of developing honesty, teamwork, communication, and positive work ethic only add to the rationale for experiential teaching and learning.

Dedication

To my grandchildren, Jackson and Ruby.
It is my hope that they have teachers who help them reach their potential by enriching their education with quality experiential based learning.

Acknowledgments

Ten years ago, I conducted my first activities workshop for a group of school council advisers. Prior to that time, I had been an educator for 25 years. From that first workshop opportunity, **Energizer Olson Presentations** was born. I did not set out to create a speaking and training business. I had no idea that I would publish a book or present to over 200,000 people. This whole experience has evolved as a labor of love, dedicated to improve teaching and learning, and energizing all types of groups.

My basic goal with **Energizer Olson Presentations** is to make a difference by bringing energy and ideas to those groups to which I am privileged to present. This second book is an outgrowth of this success.

There are many people to thank for the growth of my business and the completion of this book. My wife, Kathy, is the heart and soul of what has been accomplished. She keeps the books and handles details that would bog me down. Her efforts free me up to be creative and energetic. We are a great team. Kathy is the best thing that ever happened to me.

Our children Nick, Katie and Patrick allowed me to grow up with them. They always enjoyed having us as part of their lives. There is still a lot of kid in me. I know my children will always encourage me to bring my kid out to play. I now have two grandchildren. I am excited to continue to play along with them as they grow and change.

John Schieffer, my principal at Barron High School in 1974, suggested that I become a student council adviser. John is the best educational leader with whom I have ever worked. John saw something in me that I did not see in myself. His suggestion set in motion the current direction of my life. Other colleagues agree that we experienced something special interacting with him. Thank you, John.

In my first book, I made a special note to thank Earl Rehum and Don Larsen for their encouragement. Earl and Don have been giants in leadership education. I am very fortunate to have worked with them. Don passed away this winter, and all of us that were touched by him feel a sense of loss. In his seventies, Earl continues to inspire others, and hopefully will continue his magic for years to come.

Special people who have influenced me include my friends from youth leadership and the Wisconsin Association of School Councils. Patty Hupfer-Riedel and her sister, Anne Stevenson, have been great friends and supporters. Roger Chambers followed Don Larsen as the executive director of the WASC. I feel fortunate for his trust and confidence.

By interacting with me, many people have stimulated the energy I possess. The name *"Energizer"* describes who I am and how I approach my work. We all need to be energized in order to keep fresh and positive. We need to be aware of our surroundings and the people we meet because they are the best teachers. These day-to-day interactions fuel our positive, creative desire to grow and improve.

I cannot conclude my thank you list without mentioning Educational Media Corporation®, the publisher of my books. The owners, Don and Earl Sorenson, have acted as my guides and counselors as I grow and expand in this business. I have only been doing this on an active level for a short time, but these two have spent a lifetime mentoring people in counseling and guidance as they publish their ideas. They do their work with professional will and personal humility. If you have any ideas concerning how to improve teaching and learning, you should contact Educational Media Corporation® as a potential publisher.

About the Author:
Carl *"Energizer"* Olson

Carl Olson is a life long educator and advocate for the experiential learning theory. His previous book, *"Energizers: Calisthenics for the Mind,"* will soon be in its fourth printing. His books supplement his workshops and training sessions.

Carl's professional background includes a master's degree in education from Minnesota State University at Winona and a master's degree in guidance and counseling from Wisconsin State University—Stout. He also has experience and certification as a school administrator K-12. In addition, Carl has over 30 years of involvement in leadership education. This comes from his work as a student council adviser, Wisconsin Association of School Councils board member, leadership camp director, and presenter at various conferences and workshops. On the national level, Carl served as an adviser for the National Association of School Councils Leadership Training Center. He was also the director of the adult N.L.C. program for five years. In 2003, he was voted the first ever National Middle School Adviser of the Year.

He has won numerous other awards including:

2002 National Association of School Councils
Region 4 Earl Rehum Leadership Award

1998 Wisconsin Association of School Councils
Leadership Award

1996 Wisconsin Association of School Councils
State Adviser of the Year

1996 Wisconsin Association of School Councils
Candidate for the National Adviser of the Year

1994 Wisconsin Association of School Councils
Meritorious Service Award

1979 Barron Area School **Teacher of the Year**

Energizer Olson Presentations

663 Clardell Drive
Sun Prairie, Wisconsin 53590
Ph.: 608-318-0307 Fax: 608-318-0308
www.energizerolson.com
carl@energizerolson.com
Energetic, Informative, Inspirational
" Message with Magic"

I. Speaking Engagements:

Keynote addresses	Lunch/dinner speeches
Student lyceums	Convention breakouts
Training sessions	Workshop presentations
Corporate groups	Youth groups
Government offices	Health care personnel
Graduations	Awards banquets

All ages and any size group—we work with you to design the most effective presentation.

Topics Include:

Leadership, Character, Team Building, Communications, Problem Solving, Customer Service, Self-improvement, Education Activities, A.O.D.A. issues, and more.

II. Teaching & Training Supplies:

E.O.P. stocks and markets products for use in effective presentations. These products have been tried and tested with all types of groups. Products include high quality books, user-friendly magic tricks, and training manipulatives. All items are reasonably priced and relate to activities presented in the E.O.P. books. See www.energizerolson.com for ordering information.

"Make it big, do it right, give it class, and wrap it with love."

P.T. Barnum

Carl Olson

Part 1 • Energizers

Activities designed to activate the emotional nature of the group. The energizer can be directly related to the educational objective being presented or simply act as a mood enhancement vehicle. This type of activity is most often short and works well as an introduction tool.

All Tied Up

History: I am very fortunate to meet and learn from people as I travel around presenting and training. In doing these presentations, I meet people who give me additional ideas. People who are activity-orientated are always excited to share ideas. I got this particular idea at a conference I was doing in Eau Claire, Wisconsin. I had just finished a workshop and a man came up to me and shared this activity. I did not get his name, but I have used the activity many times with great effectiveness. It is a little difficult to figure out, but it is fun. It always challenges the people with whom I am working. I like to use it in both large and small group settings.

Materials: All you need is one piece of string about 36 inches long. It should be tied in at the ends to form a loop. I would suggest a heavy grade of string, so your loop does not tangle.

Time: 10 minutes

Group Size: Any size

Description: The object of the trick is to weave your hand through the loop, giving the impression you are binding it around your hand. You make two passes through the loop and finish by pulling your hand downward. In doing this, the hand that seemed to be tied up is actually free from the loop.

　　　　　　　　　　　　Carl Olson

The trick is done in the following steps:

1. Hold the loop on the top, letting it hang down.

2. Take your free hand from outside the loop and have it pass through it toward your body.

3. Once your hand is through the loop, turn your thumb downward and have that hand go around the edge of the loop away from it.

4. As your hand goes around the loop, have your thumb catch the loop and pull it back towards your body.

5. Now have your hand go back through the loop and pull it down in one move.

It would seem that in this process you have tied your hand up, but in fact it is free. I get the best results when I demonstrate the trick and follow it by giving everyone a piece of string. I do this toward the end of my presentation so the participants can be assigned the task of learning how to do it. The next time I see them, we review the trick and follow it by showing them how it is done. This method holds the group in suspense until the trick is learned.

Diversity Mixer

History: I do not remember when I learned this technique, but it was most likely used in one of my college classes. This is a simple activity that lends itself to group understanding.

Materials: None

Time: 10 minutes

Group Size: Any number

Description: When we think of diversity, we think of differences in terms of race, sexuality, religion or even economic position. It is a goal of many to break down these barriers and increase human understanding. I believe diversity and the grouping of people is much more complex than the visible differences we find in each other. In my years of working with all types and ages of people, I have found that all people seek a comfort level and they feel the most safe when they are with their friends. Everyone needs friends and, of course, friendship is important.

Friendship can limit us, however. If we only move toward and with our friends, it hinders our ability to expand and discover what other people in our surroundings have to offer. I lived in a small town where everyone seemed to know everything about each other. What I have found is people develop strong friendships, yet the peer groups that form are just as limiting as groups in larger cities. This activity is designed to use peer groups to bring about understanding.

To begin the activity, I ask the participants to form groups. The number in each group determines the number of groups I want to work with in my activity. If I want a total of four groups, I have the participants form groups of four. This is always done quickly as people will most likely find a group of four friends.

Next, I have them decide, in their groups, who will have one of four labels. An example would be for the group members to assign themselves the labels of north, south, east and west. Again this is easy for the groups to do. At this point, I instruct them to regroup according to their labels.

The new groups will then work together in the day's lesson or task. In this activity, I use friendships to move people away from what is safe and comfortable and I force them to work with individuals outside their peer group.

Learning Connections: Diversity should always be part of our planning when we are working with groups. The more we can open up understanding of all people in our lives, the more our horizons expand.

Hot Rod /
Paddle Move

History: This is an old magic trick. The paddle move is an easy to do basic slight of hand technique. It is best done close up with small groups of people. The total routine also uses the magic concept of forced choice.

Materials: A paddle move stick is needed. A *Fan-ta-stick* is included in the *Impact Pak*. I have seen them also called, *Hot Rods* or *Jumping Gems.* These can be purchased from most magic shops. You can make your own using wood, plastic and stickers. You would need to apply the stickers the same way the marks are on the commercially produced models.

Time: 0-5 minutes

Group Size: Works best with small groups up to 5 people.

Description: The paddle move stick is shown with different objects or sides visible to the person(s) with whom you are working. It is best done in smaller groups, as the object itself is not large enough to present to more than a few people gathered around you. You start by showing the one side, then pretend to turn it over, showing the other side. The paddle move allows you to give the impression you are turning it over. The paddle move is done by rotating the object one half turn as you move it from side to side or up and down.

There are six different objects on the rod, so you ask a person you have chosen to give you a number between one and six. Note that the key object you want that person to choose is third from the end and fourth from your hand. This is the point where you apply the forced choice principle. Use the following sequence to get your desired answer:

Choice	Method
#1	SPELL ONE FROM END
#2	SPELL TWO FROM END
#3	COUNT 1-2-3 FROM END
#4	SPELL FOUR FROM HAND
#5	SPELL FIVE FROM HAND
#6	SPELL SIX FROM END

Using this method, you will always end up at the desired object or color. At that point, you simply turn over the object and say, "Look, now they are all that shape or color."

Again, using the paddle move, you can show that both sides are the same. All you are doing is the paddle move on the other side.

This is one magic trick that cannot be examined or handed out for inspection. After you do the trick, simply put it in your pocket and answer their questions, using the magicians magic words. When asked how did you do that, you respond, "Very well, thank you!"

Learning Connections: I like this trick because it works well for people of all ages. It is quick and easy to do, and it can easily be carried in your pocket. It is a great opener/ ice breaker.

Rubber Band Jump

History: This is a simple old magic trick/ stunt. It is easy to do and fun to share with people. It works well with younger children.

Materials: One rubber band of medium size. I like to use bands of different colors to create a better effect.

Time: 10-20 minutes

Group Size: Can be used with individual students and up to a classroom-sized group.

Description: Hold your hand out with your palm facing toward you. Drape the rubber band over your fingers, as shown. The band goes over your index finger and middle finger. The next step is to make a fist by closing your fingers. Then, pull the band over all of your finger tips. After the band is secure over your finger tips, quickly straighten out your fingers and the band will change places. This can also be done with two rubber bands by placing the second rubber band over your ring and little finger.

Learning Connections: This is another trick I do to catch people's attention. It is another good conversation starter and it gives you the chance to share.

String Escape

History: I learned this activity from a counselor friend of mine at a summer leadership camp. It is a good beginning magic trick. I like to use it with younger children. It can be done close up or in front of large groups.

Materials: A 24 to 32-inch piece of good quality string. Tie the ends together to make one big loop. The object is to make the string penetrate through solid objects. Many times I will wear the string loop around my neck. When asked what it is for, I have the ideal lead in for the trick.

Time: 10-20 minutes

Group Size: Any size group.

Description: Stretch the string loop between your thumbs. Pull the string loop through or around any solid object. The completion of the trick requires you do two simple moves. The moves are done quickly.

When done well, it will appear the string has gone through the solid object.

The two moves are as follows:

1. First, take your right hand and reach around the string held by the left thumb. Hook the string with your index finger.

2. Second, make the same move with the opposite hand.

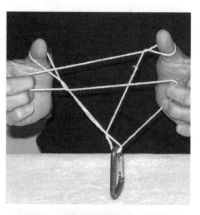

You will now be holding the string with both thumbs and both index fingers. To complete the trick, quickly pull on the string, stretching it out. In the process of pulling it, let go with one of your thumbs and let go with the index finger on the opposite hand. This will leave you holding the string with one index finger and one

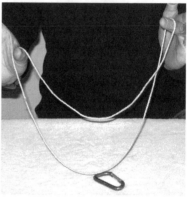

thumb. In the process of this pulling move, your string actually goes around the solid object, but it gives the illusion of penetrating it.

I like to have someone hold out an arm and I make the string go through it. This is a good effect for younger children.

Learning Connections: I use this activity as a conversation starter. It helps me make connections with the people. It is also a good lead in to the topic of trust. An example would be: *"It takes trust for you to let me pull this string through your arm."*

Unlock Your Potential

History: This is a small hand-held trick that can be done close-up or with larger groups. I learned it at a wellness conference. After my presentation, a lady came up to me and said that she had a trick to share with me. I listened and learned, and now I use the activity in many situations.

Materials: You will need two 2- to 2.5-inch objects (example, straws, dowel rods, corks). The objects need to be long and slim. They need to be easily held between your thumb and index finger. I have found using two different colored objects adds to the effect.

Time: 10-20 minutes

Group Size: Any size group. All participants will need a set of the objects for the trick.

Description: Start by showing the two objects. Put the objects in the beginning position, holding them in the space between 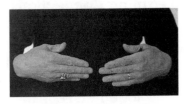 your thumbs and index fingers. The goal of the trick is to have the objects switch places. Using your thumb and index finger from each hand, try to take the object from one hand to the other. This must be done so both objects are moved at the same time.

The problem that people encounter at this point is they almost always end up with their hands still connected together by the two objects. In order to accomplish the trick without having your hands still connected, the following steps have to be taken.

1. Hold the objects in the standing position as shown in the first picture.

2. Turn your hands so that they are facing each other with one thumb pointing up and one down.

3. With the back hand, reach over your front thumb and secure the object with your thumb and index finger.

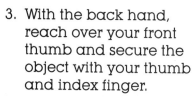

4. The other thumb is placed on top of the other object, while you secure the other end of that object with your free index finger.

5. At this point you pull the two objects apart.

6. Then place them back in the same position to complete the trick.

Learning Connections: I can easily carry these objects in my pocket. This allows me to use the trick as an introduction tool.

I start by defining the problem of moving the objects from hand to hand without getting tied together. I ask the group to do it at the same time I demonstrate it. Even though they can see me do it, most will struggle.

Next, I go through it again slowly, with a more detailed explanation. Through trial and error, the individuals or group will find success. It works well to have the people who are successful model their understanding for others. The activity to reinforce concepts such as:

1. Unlocking your potential.

2. Working together for success.

3. Simple things are sometimes difficult.

Positive Energy

Materials: One *Energy Ball* per group. One is included in the *Impact Pak*.

Time: 10-15 minutes

Group Size: 1-25 participants, any age group.

Description: The object of this activity is to show the power that groups have when they work together. It also shows how important personal connections are when we are trying to work together to accomplish tasks.

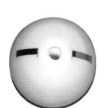

Arrange the group in a circle. They can be standing, seated in chairs or on the floor. Explain to the group that you want to show the effect of using our positive energy when we work together. Start by holding the energy ball with one hand and touching one of the metal circuit points with your index finger. Then use your other index finger to touch the index finger of the person next to you. That person uses their other index finger to connect to the person next to them and so on around the circle. The connection is complete when the last person touches the other metal circuit point with their index finger. When the circuit is complete, the ball will light up and make a beeping sound. If anyone breaks the circuit anywhere in the circle, the light will go out. The idea is that great things happen when everyone in the group uses their positive energy. A group will not succeed if people disconnect to leave others to do all the work.

Brain Storming Ball

History: There are practical tools to use for group interaction all around us. The flashing ball is a good example. This ball flashes for 15 seconds each time it is bounced. It can be used as a tool for brainstorming.

Materials: All you need is a *Flashing Ball*. One is included in the *Impact Pak*. These can be purchased at various places listed in the resources section at the back of this book.

Description: Group order or the art of taking turns is always a consideration when working with a number of participants. The goal of this activity is to get as many ideas as possible, while keeping the discussion organized and, at the same time, giving all parties a chance to participate. The rules for brainstorming are very simple. The group goal is to get as many ideas as possible in a preset time period. All reasonable ideas relating to the topic or goal are accepted.

The blinking ball is a tool for this activity because it allows only one person to talk at a time within a limited time frame. The time frame is the 15 seconds that the ball blinks.

Learning Connections: We must respect everyone's opinion. By allowing only the person with the ball to speak, this concept is reinforced. Limiting each person to 15 seconds requires the speaker to get to the point. In some cases, I have allowed two or three bounces to give the speaker more time.

Focus Wheel

History: This is a
magic trick that
I have adapted
for teaching. It
has many appli-
cations. I use it
as a metaphor
for the idea of
being focused
and staying
zoned in on
what we want to
accomplish. I
have known
science teachers who use it when teaching
about the eye and the muscles that control it.
The wheel creates an illusion that is sure to be
a showstopper.

Materials: You will need a *Focus Wheel*. See
www.energizerolson.com for ordering information. Along with the focus wheel, you also
will need a watch with a second hand on it.

Time: 5-15 minutes

Group Size: Any number. (I have done this with as
many as two thousand people. The farther
back the participants are, the better the trick
works.)

Description: To get the desired effect, instruct the group to stare at the very center of the focus wheel while it is spinning. Have them stare at it for thirty seconds, while you time them and encourage them. For the last five seconds, let them know that you will count down 5, 4, 3, 2, 1. When you get to one, have them look at your nose. Depending on the direction the wheel is spinning, your head will appear to either expand or contract. The effect will last for just a few seconds, but it is startling and immediate. This works for any sized group. The participants should be at least fifteen feet away and have a clear view of the wheel.

Learning Connections: At this point, I would review the effect. I had asked the audience to really "focus," and the result was perceiving a definite change in my head. I then go back to the idea of being focused, and how we can accomplish many things when we are focused. If they can focus and perceive that my head got bigger or smaller, they should be able to apply this ability to concentrate to do any of the following:

1. Be a good friend.
2. Be a good student.
3. Be a good citizen.
4. Accomplish their goals.

Giant Straw
"You don't always get what you want"

History: This is a standard magic trick with many applications. I use it for the concept of "resiliency." In all aspects of life, people have to deal with disappointment. How this is handled deter-mines our feelings and how we approach life in general. Through the use of this trick, I am able to bring this concept to a higher level of understanding. There are many other applications for this trick. It is easy to do and it can be used with any sized group.

Materials: One Giant Straw. (See www.energizerolson.com for ordering information), a bag from McDonald's and empty cartons from various McDonald's products (Chicken McNuggets, Big Mac and a small soda cup.)

Time: 5-10 minutes

Group Size: Any number. (Good large group presentation piece)

Description: Start out by showing the McDonald's bag, loaded with the empty cartons, the small soda cup and the giant straw. Tell the group you did not have time to get lunch, but you did stop at McDonald's. Ask if the group would mind if you eat and talk at the same time. Show that you have purchased some of your favorite products. One by one take the products out of the bag. Save the soda cup and the straw for last.

After you show the products, ask if the group has ever ordered something and not gotten what they wanted. In every case, this is a question to which all people can relate. You can even ask for some examples. Tell the group you asked them to super size your order. You wanted a large Coke. Take the small soda cup out of the bag and express your displeasure. Then note that not only did you get the small Coke, but they also gave you this large straw. Pull the giant straw out of the bag and wait for the group's reaction.

The point I make is the idea *"you don't always get what you want."* I asked for the large Coke and I got a small one and also I got this large straw. How do you handle it when you are rejected, discouraged or put down? We need to be resilient and find ways to deal with these types of situations.

Learning Connections: We do not always get what we want. Disappointment is, of course, a fact of life. This trick clearly illustrates this concept. It is a great opening for a discussion about this topic. People need to develop strategies to handle adversity. I use this trick to lead into a discussion on this topic.

Smile on a Stick

History: A few years ago, I was presenting at an Illinois Middle School Student Council Advisers conference where one of the advisers introduced me to the "smile on a stick." I use it as a quick energizer that is really fun.

Materials: A *Smile on a Stick* piece. See www.energizerolson.com for ordering information. They come in three colors to match the ethnicity of the facilitator. There are also frowns on a stick available (white only).

Time: 5 minutes

Group Size: Any number

Description: I carry the smile piece around with me and hold it in front of my face when I feel the group needs a boost. When you put it up to your face, or hold it up to someone else's, it generates a smile or laugh in return.

It is a great stress breaker and can be used for all age groups. Younger children really like it.

I have also used the smile on a stick as a counseling tool. If I encounter a client who is having difficulties, I give that person a smile on a stick to try it out on people the rest of the day. At the end of the day, I meet with the student and discuss the reactions received.

Air Bags

Materials: Two *Air Bags*. The *Impact Pak* includes four Air Bags.

Time: 10 to 20 minutes

Group Size: Any number—works best with 6 or more

Procedure: The entire outline and sequence is on the Air Bags Worksheet. The visual effect of this activity is very strong.

Air Bags Worksheet

Objectives:

1. To energize and heighten student interests.
2. To give a visual symbol of the concept of successful cooperation.

Procedure:

1. Ask for a student volunteer.
2. Get the volunteer's name and let that person know you are going to ask him or her to blow up a balloon. (Give the volunteer a chance to opt out at this point.)
3. After you have an agreement, unfold the air bag balloon and instruct the volunteer to blow it up while you talk. (Make sure to have the volunteer hold the air bag close to his or her mouth.)
4. While the volunteer is working, talk to the group, making the following points:

   a. We need to get adequate information before making a quick decision.

   b. It is also important that we know if the task we undertake is possible with the resources we have.

5. Show the class that the end of the bag is open so it is impossible to blow it up.
6. Suggest a contest between the volunteer and yourself. Tie the ends of the bags. Stand back to back and have additional volunteers hold the bags out horizontally from the contestants' mouths. Give the "Ready, set, go" command and start the contest.

NOTE: The secret move is to hold your bag away from your face and blow directly at the bag opening. If done correctly, you should fill the bag with one breath. Close the end and hold your full bag while the volunteer puffs away. (This will bring a big laugh from the observers.)

7. Thank the volunteer. Have that person sit down and ask the following questions.

Processing Questions:

1. How did I set up the volunteer for failure?

2. Are there situations in our everyday life where people do this same thing to us? Where and when does this happen to us?

3. What did I do differently when I blew up the balloon? *(1. I held the mouth of the balloon open 2. I blew from a distance)*

4. Why is it important to keep an open mind as we make decisions?

5. When I blow from a distance, I am using my own air and the air pressure around me. In doing this I am using all my resources. What resources do we have that help make us successful?

6. What is a mentor? Why is it important to cultivate and use mentors in our life?

Are You Sound Minded?

History: I first started teaching in 1968. The person who held the job before me left a number of files. This activity was in the file of materials and I have used it many times over the course of my teaching career.

Materials: Each participant needs the worksheet entitled: *"R Use Hound Mine Dead?"* You will have another similar sheet containing the answers.

Time: 15-20 minutes

Group Size: Any number

Description: The object of the game is to have the group figure out the solution, or correct question or statement, to each of the clues. All of the clues are commonly heard and used. This activity is enjoyable as well as challenging. Notice that the title at the top of the worksheet to be handed out is: "R Use Hound Mine Dead?"

The name of the actual activity is ***"Are You Sound Minded?"*** This activity works most successfully with adults. It can be used with students, but adaptations are necessary. These are some of the strategies that I used.

1. Introduce two or three of the clues each day and give extra credit for anyone who can figure them out. Encourage the students to involve their parents or family members and report back on who helped them solve the problem. In doing this, you can find out which students received help at home and which ones are motivated to do extra work for class projects.

2. Another way to use this activity is to give out the answers and have the group try to match the answers with the clues. When you do this, hand out the answers randomly so the participants will have to search and think, rather than find things in simple order.

This is an excellent icebreaker which creates laughter and conversation when used with adult groups. Hand out the list and have individuals, pairs, or groups try to figure out the answers. The process of figuring out the answers builds team spirit and stimulates problem solving thinking.

R Use Hound Mine Dead?

1. ROCKER BUY BAY BEE INNER TREAT HOP.
2. PADDER KEY PADDER KEG PRGGERS MENG.
3. TURNIP OUTS FIR PLY.
4. ROLANDS TONE GADDERS NOME SHES.
5. SINKERS HONKERS SICK SPENTS.
6. LOW TENT BRITCHES FULL IN TOWN.
7. DIAMOND DIED WEIGHTS FOR NOME ANN.
8. BUT TUNE TOOT A GATHER.
9. MY TEA HOAX FARM LEDLE EGGS HORNS CROW.
10. HIGH PLED JELLY GENTS TWO THELF LAG.
11. A FIT FURS CHEWED OWN SUCK SEED DRY EGG HEN.
12. WENT A DRAIN SIT BORES.
13. THOROUGHLY BURT GASHES SWARM.
14. BUTTER LAY DONE EVER.
15. ALL SWELL ATTEND SWELL.
16. HUM TEDIUM TES SET HONOR WOOL.
17. UP ANY SHAVED SUP ANY URNED.
18. ASHER WAIT A BULBV BOUNCES.
19. INK OUT WEED RUST.
20. A NAP A LAD KEYS A DECK TRAY WEIGH.
21. KEY PASS TIFF UP HURL LIP.
22. AIR SNOW FULL IKE KNOWL FULL.
23. HULKING COAL VASSAR MURRAY HOLTZ HOLE.
24. AL WAITS BEAP A LIGHT.
25. BURDEN HEN SWART TUNA PUSH.
26. ROW MUSN'T BILL TINTED "A".
27. HAVE FELLOW FIZZ GED (BED?) AIR A NUN.

R Use Hound Mine Dead? ANSWERS

1. ROCK A BYE BABY IN THE TREE TOP.
2. PADDY CAKE PADDY CAKE BAKERS MAN.
3. TURN ABOUT IS FAIR PLAY.
4. A ROLLING STONE GATHERS NO MOSS.
5. SING A SONG OF SIXPENCE.
6. LONDON BRIDGES FALLING DOWN.
7. TIME WAITS FOR NO MAN.
8. PUT TWO AND TWO TOGETHER.
9. MIGHTY OAKS FROM LITTLE ACORN GROW.
10. PLEDGE ALLEGIANCE TO THE FLAG.
11. IF AT FIRST YOU DON'T SUCCEED TRY TRY AGAIN.
12. WHEN IT RAINS IT POURS.
13. THE EARLY BIRD GETS THE WORM.
14. BETTER LATE THAN NEVER.
15. ALL'S WELL THAT ENDS WELL.
16. HUMPTY DUMPTY SAT ON THE WALL.
17. DON'T LEAVE ANY STONE UNTURNED.
18. THAT'S THE WAY THE BALL BOUNCES.
19. IN GOD WE TRUST.
20. AN APPLE A DAY KEEPS THE DOCTOR AWAY.
21. KEEP A STIFF UPPER LIP.
22. THERE IS NO FOOL LIKE AN OLD FOOL.
23. OLD KING COLE WAS A MERRY OLD SOUL.
24. ALWAYS BE POLITE.
25. A BIRD IN THE HAND IS WORTH TWO IN THE BUSH
26. ROME WASN'T BUILT IN A DAY.
27. HALF A LOAF IS BETTER THAN NONE.

Floating Cup Trick

History: Dr. Earl Reum is one of my greatest mentors and source of materials. I first saw this trick done by him and I have used it ever since. It is a quick and easy stunt that gets the group's attention and makes a good transition activity.

Materials: One styrofoam or paper cup with a small hole cut in the side.

Time: 5 minutes

Group Size: Any number

Description: Hold the cup with one hand underneath it and the other hand behind it. The audience will not see your ring finger in the hole in the cup. Tell the group you want to show them your famous magic floating cup trick. Have them say some magic word or count to three. At this point, drop your hand from below the cup and straighten out your fingers. The ring finger

will be holding the cup. You can even wiggle it back and forth to add to the effect.

There is no great secret to this magic trick. The main object is to create some humor and use it to move from one thought process to the next. If you have time, allow the group to make their own magic cups and practice the routine. Assign them the task of doing this trick for one of their family members or co-workers. Have them report back the reactions they receive.

Mouth Coil

History: This easy magic trick requires a small amount of slight of hand. It has a great effect that will catch the audience off guard. I like to use it to begin a presentation. Using it helps me to get the audience's attention, and it sets a fun mood for the rest of my presentation.

Materials: *Mouth Coils* can be purchased from most all magic outlets.
See www.energizerolson.com for ordering information. There are many different sizes and types.

Time: 5 minutes

Group Size: Any number

Description: There are many different effects and ideas for the use of a mouth coil. The one I would suggest is as a metaphor for putting things together once they have been torn apart or confused. Start with a plain piece of tissue or a napkin. As you are talking, tear it into several pieces. While you are doing this, compare the process of tearing it to the way people will shoot down a new idea or one with which they are uncomfortable.

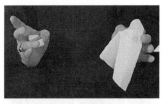

Tell the group you have a magical way to put things back together so they can be looked at differently.

All the while you are talking, you will secretly hold a mouth coil in the palm of your hand. At this point, ball up the torn pieces and put them into the same hand that holds the mouth coil. With a quick move, pop the mouth coil into your mouth, making it look like it was the ball of torn pieces. Pretend to chew and move the pieces around in your mouth, making faces

in order to attract attention to your face.

While doing this, discard the ball of torn pieces in your pocket, or anywhere that will not be noticed. After this, reach up to your mouth and begin to pull the mouth coil from your mouth. Most mouth coils are anywhere from 15 to 20 feet in length. Keep pulling and pulling with a surprised look on you face. It will be colorful and shocking for the group.

Neck Breaker

History: This attention-captur-
ing deception always gets a
good laugh. I have seen this
used by many people. It
was written up in the Penn &
Teller book, *How to Play in
Traffic.* It is a good presentation transition to either
start, end or bridge be-
tween concepts. I have used
this activity many times to
facilitate these efforts.

Materials: One hard plastic cup
(8 oz.)

Time: 5 minutes

Group Size: Any number

Description: Put a plastic cup
under your arm out of sight
of the group to whom you
are talking. Tell the group
that you need to straighten
a few things out before they
begin work. At that point,

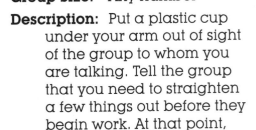

take both hands and grab your head while
holding the cup under your arm. Twist your
head toward the side where the cup is being
held. Apply pressure to the cup, causing it to
break and make a loud cracking sound.
Shake your head and say now it is time to get
down to work. I like to show that I had the cup
under my arm.

The most important thing that has happened is
you have focused the group's attention on you.

Nose Breaker

History: I learned this trick from one of my students. It is an attention getter and I use it just for fun.

Materials: None

Description: You simply put both of your hands over your nose and move them from one side to the other, giving the impression you are moving your nose. At the same time, you use one of your thumbs to make a snapping sound. This is done by hooking one of your thumbnails behind your front teeth and pulling forward. This action is hidden behind your hands and it makes it seem like you are cracking your nose, much the same way you would crack your knuckles.

I like to use this activity to attract attention and get a reaction out of people. It always seems to get a good laugh and is good active fun.

Show'em Your Smarts

History: I saw this gag done at a play called *Triple Espresso*. They used it for humor, and I have adopted it as a way of breaking the ice and establishing rapport with a group. I use it as a kickoff to a lesson. It is fun and always captures the group's attention. I believe humor has a place in teaching and learning. Good teachers or presenters need to be able to have a bag of tricks to charge things up. This would be an example of that type of activity.

Materials: A clear plastic sheet protector with two pages in it. On one side there is a large question mark visible. On the other side would be the word NO. Inside the sheet protector, between the two pages, you have three sheets of paper with pictures of pigs on them. To set up the trick, put the pig pictures in the sheet holder hidden by the two cover sheets.

Time: 10 minutes

Group Size: Any number

Description: Pick out a volunteer
and have that person come to
the front of the group. Tell the
group that you are going to
show them how smart the
volunteer is. Hold the sheet
holder against your body,
showing only the question
mark. Do not let anyone see
the other side of the prop. Ask

this question of the volunteer: "Do you know
the word on the other side of this sheet? Answer yes or no." They will always respond "NO"
and, at that point, turn it over to show the
word NO. You can say," See how smart you
are!"

This will always get some
laughs. Next, put one of your
hands in the plastic sheet
holder in between the two
papers.

Then ask the volunteer to give
you a number between one
and five. After the answer is
given, pull out your hand and
hold up the number of fingers
to match the answer.

Once again, this will get some good laughs.
Lastly, ask the volunteer to name a farm animal. When the animal is named, regardless of
what is said, pull out a pig card. Show the
group and repeat the question and process
until all three pig cards have been shown.
This activity gets a lot of laughs, no matter
what animals are mentioned. However, it is
funniest when the volunteer guesses the pig
last because of catching on to the prank.

The More You Know the Better

History: I first saw this being done by a magician and speaker named Russ Peak. Russ presents to a wide variety of groups. When I saw him do this, we were both working for a Minnesota State school secretary's conference. You can find contact information about Russ in the resources section at the back of this book.

Materials: None

Time: 5 minutes

Group Size: Any number

Description: This is a very simple trick that is a great lead in to a discussion about the importance of getting all the necessary information. You start by asking the group to hold out one arm with an open hand and thumb pointing down.

Next, have them bring their other arm forward, reaching over and across their first arm and clasping their hands together.

Now, you quickly unclasp your top arm and point to someone in the group as if you are giving them directions. Then quickly bring your hand forward, but this time reach under your top hands and clasp. Lastly, ask the group to copy you as you turn your hands up so that your thumbs are pointing upward.

They will not be able to do it, as their hands are in a position that will not allow them to do it. This always gets a good laugh. You can repeat the whole process again and then make the point that they are unable to do this and you can because you know information they do not. Lastly, show them what you did and have them experience success by doing the trick your way.

Learning Connections: Processing questions:

1. What did it feel like to do the trick without knowing the correct way?
2. Did the activity seem difficult?
3. How did the people around you react?
4. Did the people around you offer any help in solving the problem?
5. How did it feel to do the activity when you had all the necessary information?
6. How is this similar to real life situations in which we find ourselves?
7. What are some actions we can take to avoid this type of problem or frustration?

Point of View

History: I was introduced to this activity at a staff inservice program I was conducting in Maple Grove, Minnesota. I do not remember the name of the staff member that showed me the activity, but I have found it to be a simple idea which has powerful meaning. It shows the importance of looking at ideas through differing perspectives. I have used it many times with adults as well student groups.

Materials: None

Time: 5 minutes

Group Size: Any number

Description: Have the people with whom you are working hold one hand at waist level with their index finger pointing towards the ceiling. Tell them to move their index finger in a clockwise direction, without stopping.

Have them raise their heads and look straight ahead. Instruct them not to look up or down; they are to look straight ahead, keeping their  eyes level. During the whole activity, they are to continue to circle their finger in that same clockwise direction.

Next, have them move their finger upwards, while they are doing the original motion. They should continue to move the circling finger upwards until it is well above their head. At this point, have them look up and see what direction their finger is rotating. They will notice at waist level it was clockwise and now above their heads, it will be going counterclockwise.

The name of this activity is "Point of View." On most issues, people will have different points of view. In this case, just by moving to a different level we get the opposite action. It all depends on your point of view.

Learning Connections: Seeing all sides of an issue and respecting the diversity of human thought is a job we as educators are challenged to do. I like this activity because it is a practical application of an attitude we would like to develop in our students. I like to introduce it at the beginning of a study and then keep referring to it when greater understanding is needed.

Expand Your Possibilities

History: Many of the activities in this book come from science experiments. Magician's use science principals like this one to help create illusions. In this activity, I combine water with a polymer to create the metaphors of personal expansion and positive changes. I first saw this material being demonstrated by Steve Spangler of *Steve Spangler Science*. See the resources section at the back of this book for more information on Steve and his work.

Materials: A small amount of the polymer, *"Snow,"* water and a clear glass. *Snow* is included in the *Impact Pak*.

I find that two to three teaspoons of the polymer combined with eight ounces of water make an effective presentation piece. You will also need a tray or some other container to catch the excess materials as the polymer and the water react.

Time: 5 minutes

Group Size: Any number

Description: I use this activity as either an opening or a closing demonstration. I use it to reinforce the concept of expanding possibilities and making positive changes. This can be used to refer to individuals or an organization. I make the point that all of us have strong personal attributes we need to share or develop. I compare the small amount of white powder and the glass of water to those qualities. I note our positive qualities need to be developed and shared in order to get the maximum results. I then pour the water into the glass with the white powder and allow the chemical reaction to occur.

If I use it at the opening of a presentation, I leave the material in plain view. During my talk, I keep referring to the concepts I am trying to make. It works great to grab a handful of the snow and let it fall back onto the tray or receptacle as you continue to reinforce the points of the presentation.

When I use it to end a presentation, I use it to add one more comparison to the topic I am presenting. I do allow participants to handle the final material, but I note they should wash their hands before eating, as this is a chemical. It should not be ingested.

Learning Connections: The polymer powder can be compared to the natural talents all of us have. The water represents ways we can enhance these talents. Left alone, there would be just powder and water, but combined together, the powder expands and makes positive changes, just like we would want our talents to develop and change.

Mind Power

History: I am not sure where I first saw this activity. It is an old standby with good application to learning situations. It works off the power of suggestion. It is fun and is easy to set up and deliver.

Materials: Each participant must have:

1. A metal washer

2. A piece of string or yarn 24 inches long

3. A piece of paper marked as in the photo

Time: 15-20 minutes

Description: Have each participant tie the string to the washer so that they have approximately 18 inches of string left to hold. Next have each person set the paper down so that the compass marks are in the correct direction. They should hold the end of the their string high enough so the washer is about one inch from the surface of the paper. They then dangle the washer as still as possible directly above the center point of the drawing.

The participants should attempt to keep their washer motionless. As the holders are concentrating on holding their washer steady, verbally suggest that they think of one of the directions on the drawing—either north to south or east to west. Loud enough so that all can hear you, keep saying and suggesting one of the directions. Say things like:

1. "Everyone thinks north to south, north to south, north to south."

2. "Keep the washer steady, but think north to south, north to south."

In nearly all cases, this suggestion procedure will cause the holder to move the washer in the suggested direction, even though they are trying to hold it still. It seems that the subconscious mind picks up on the thought being heard and takes over. It makes for a good discussion on how we are affected by both positive and negative suggestions.

Learning Connections: There are many forces that try to influence us at all times. Messages are sent to us through the media and from person to person. This activity shows the effect hearing the messages can have on us. Even though we try to keep the washer still, the message sent from the teacher can cause us to duplicate the action of the message.

550

History: Activities have many uses in the educational process. As I have noted earlier, activities can serve as warm-ups to learning or as transitions when moving from one concept or mode to another. I recommend this one for transition and as a warm-up energizer.

Materials: I like to use an overhead projector to show how this activity works. It can also be done on a blackboard or on a PowerPoint slide.

Time: 5 -10 minutes

Description: Put the following formula on the overhead or blackboard.

$$5 + 5 + 5 = 550$$

Ask the group to draw one line to make the statement correct. Note, they are not allowed to change the equals sign. I have them work on their own and follow up with small groups. The answer is as follows:

$$5 \, 4 \, 5 + 5 = 550$$

In order for this to work, you simply add one line to the plus sign making it a 4. Five hundred and forty five plus five equals five hundred and fifty.

Learning Connection: This is another example of a simple problem group members will need to think outside the box to solve. It works well as another introductory activity.

Bounce Back

History: I was introduced to this activity by Steve Spangler of *Steve Spangler Science*. Steve is an accomplished speaker and trainer. For more information about Steve, refer to the resources section at the back of this book. This activity creates an effective metaphor for resiliency. The activity involves such a small amount of slight of hand that it can be easily learned.

Materials: The trick uses three objects, two balls that look alike and a popper. While the balls look alike, they are different in that one of them will bounce when dropped and the  other does not bounce when dropped, but lays flat. See www.energizerolson.com for ordering information on purchasing the balls and the popper.

Time: 10 - 20 minutes

Group Size: 10 - 30 participants

Description: In this activity, you talk about the concept of resiliency. In your right hand, hold the bounce ball and in your left hand hold the no bounce ball. Your objective is to have the audience or group think you only have the bounce ball in your hands. Start by bouncing the real bounce ball and talk about how important it is to have the ability to bounce back from adversity. Always use the right hand to bounce the ball, but always catch it in the left hand with the extra ball in it.

After you have demonstrated the bouncing ball

a number of times, secretly make the switch and try to bounce the no bounce ball. Note, this ball falls flat, which is not the kind of reaction we want to adversity. In the process of the discussion, you can continue to switch the balls to show the value of having the ability to be resilient and how good it feels to "bounce back."

After this demonstration, put the balls in your pocket and suggest to the audience that they might need another approach to adversity. Take out the popper and explain that people need to summon all their inner strengths and resources in order to take a different approach. Compare possible life problems to the popper. Show that you are changing the shape of it, just like you would suggest people need to change their attitudes and efforts.

Drop the popper and it will spring back with immediate force. Discuss how this ability to change form is like our ability to be resilient. More discussion can follow this, if necessary.

Learning Connection:

Life is a series of up and down moments or experiences. How we handle these situations and what we learn from them is the key to our growth and success.

The three objects are metaphors for the whole topic of adversity. The bounce ball is compared to the way we want our students to handle difficulties. We want them to bounce back, just like the bounce ball does. The no bounce ball is compared to the wrong way to react. Finally, in order for the popper to work, it has to make changes and the result is a strong reaction. This is, of course, the type of reaction desired in successful situations.

D'lite

History: This is a popular magic trick used as an attention getter. It was created by a magician named Rocco and is available from most magic sites.

Materials: The *D'lite* kit comes with the specially designed thumb tip and instructions. See www.energizerolson.com for ordering information.

Description: You need to keep the thumb tip somewhere out of sight. Your pocket would work, or any other place where you can easily take it on and off without being noticed. Start the trick by putting on the thumb tip. Activate the light in the tip by pinching your thumb and index finger together. You can pretend to take the light out of a participant's ear. Also, I like to pretend to put the light into someone's hand and have that person throw it to me. When it is thrown, I activate the light as I pretend to catch it. There are numerous activities you can devise with this trick. In all cases, it brings focus to the group.

If you have two of the thumb tips, you can pretend to play catch with the light.

This works well with younger audiences.

Magic Archs

Materials: One set of plastic colored *Magic Archs*. See www.energizerolson.com for ordering information.

Time: 15 - 20 minutes

Description: Start by showing the arches, one at a time. Note the differences in color and the sameness of their shapes. I use the archs to make a comparison of the diversity of people. We are, of course, different races, religions, ages and sexes. Next, I show the arches together, putting one on top of the other. I ask which it larger. The illusion will cause the group to see that the top arch looks smaller. Switch the positions of the arches and ask which seems bigger now. The illusion will make the other arch seem larger. Now, cross the arches to make an X, and lastly show them end to end in the shape of an equals sign.

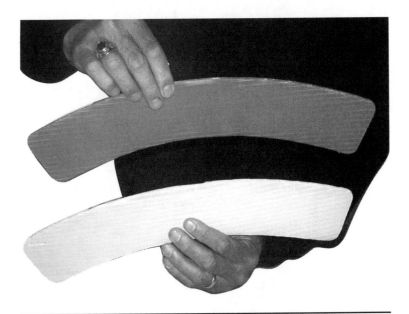

The different positions that I mentioned are metaphors for the concepts of:

1. Personal and individual differences because of the colors of the arches.
2. Discrimination and as many in society view people differently even though we are all created equally.
3. The fact that we need to work hard to multiply our possibilities.
4. We need to look at each other as equals in order to make positive advancements.

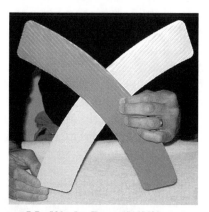

Multiply Possibilities

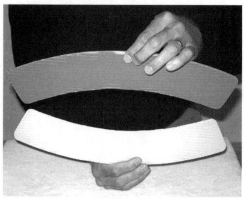

Equal Understanding

Reach Beyond

History: Bill Collar is an accomplished speaker and trainer. We have worked together on projects. I saw him do this activity at a sportsmanship workshop where we presented to a group of young athletes.

Materials: Roll of masking tape

Time: 15 - 20 minutes

Group Size: Any number

Description: For this activity, you need to select a volunteer from your group. Ask the volunteer to perform a task. The task is to stand next to the wall with both feet on the ground and reach as high as  possible on the wall. As the task is being done, stand next to the person on a chair or ladder and mark the highest point reached.

Next, have the volunteer step back. Compliment the volunteer for doing a good job. Then, notify the volunteer that you want a second try with more effort expended. When the second try is attempted, mark the highest point once again. In nearly all cases, this second attempt will surpass the first.

Learning Connection: This activity shows that we can improve our performance with practice. The standard was set the first time the activity was attempted. The goal for the second attempt was to exceed the standard. We need to practice and continue to strive for improved performance in everything we do.

Short Circuit

History: I first learned *Short Circuit* at a summer wellness conference where I was presenting. After class, a lady came up to me and shared the activity. Since that time, I have used it to make connections with people and to reinforce the concept that some things are harder than they seem.

This is an individual problem-solving activity. I have done it one on one and used it in groups where people pair up and work with each other.

Materials: None

Description: Have the persons you are working with cross their arms and lace their fingers together, as shown. Next have them bring their hands up to their faces. Make sure they grip tight as they do this exercise.

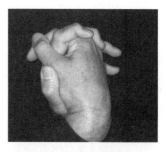

After they have their hands in this final position, point to a specific finger and ask them to move that finger. Continue to point to other fingers

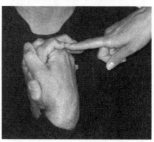

on both hands. In most cases, they will either move the wrong finger or they will not be able to move any fingers.

This shows that we are easily confused when we all under pressure or in new, confusing situations.

Carl Olson

Spring to Life

History: This trick can work for groups, but I find the best successes in small groups or one-on-one situations. It is small enough to be carried in your pocket, and it works as an icebreaker or conversation starter.

Materials: The trick consists of a four-inch loose coiled spring and a three-inch craft ring. The tension of the spring is very important. If it is too strong, you will have difficulty doing the trick. If is too loose, the trick will be too easy to figure out. A complete trick kit is available from www.energizerolson.com.

Description: Start by showing the two objects, slip the ring over the spring, and put both pieces behind your back. When it is behind your back, turn the ring a half turn clockwise and bring the spring back in front of you. At this point, the ring will be stuck on the spring. Let the participant hold and examine the spring. Take the spring back and put it behind 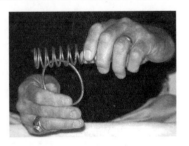 your back again. This time turn the ring the other way and bring it forward again. When you bring it forward, you will be able to take the ring off the spring. Let the participants try to duplicate what you have done. Note that they are not allowed to try and spin the ring off the spring.

Three Ropes

History: Magicians call this trick the "professor's nightmare." The trick itself takes practice, but the results are amazingly effective. It is an excellent trick to use as a metaphor for many basic concepts. I like to use it to show the importance of all people working together in a group—as a team—toward success.

Materials: Three pieces of thick, cloth rope are used in the following sizes, 33 inches, 22 inches and 11 inches. The rope should be soft and flexible.

Time: 5 -10 minutes

Group Size: Any number

Description: The rope trick can be used as a metaphor to compare three groups that live or work together. Through teamwork, their total efforts result in a strong, successful bond. When this is done for school groups, the ropes can represent the students, community and staff. The large rope is the students, because of their importance and the reason for the existence of schools. The medium rope is the community, which supports the school and the small one is the staff, which has the fewest number, yet is hugely significant.

The different sized ropes are shown and each role is talked about in relation and to success. As the discussion continues, emphasis is placed on how all groups need to work and pull together, combining ideas and efforts in order to work as a whole. The demonstrator takes the bottom of each rope and wraps it up toward the top.

While listening to the message, the group is unaware of how you, the demonstrator, is cleverly combining the ropes and pulling them together. In this action, all the ropes become the same size. Hence, the concept develops showing how all of these people have an equally important role to play.

When the activity is complete, the participants see how each group contributes equally to their organization's success, combining all of their efforts to reach the final successful goals.

The trick is setup and completed using the following steps:

1. Show the ropes one at a time and put them into your hand with your palm facing you. Start with the small rope, then the medium, and lastly the large.

2. Put them in your hand and make the ends that hang over the front of your hand the same length.

3. Next, starting with the short rope, bring the other ends of ropes up, and hang that end over your hand. All six ends will now be hanging over your hand.

4. Starting with the end farthest from you thumb, grab the first, second, and fourth rope. Pull on these ends while holding the other ends.

5. Your hand will now hold both ends of the short rope and one end of the middle rope. The other hand will hold two ends of the long rope and one of the middle rope. The long rope will be split in half by the short rope. You need to conceal this split of the long rope behind your hand.

It will look as though the ropes are now all the same length.

Learning Connection:

Each of the groups the ropes represent has important roles to play in our world. They all have strengths and weaknesses but working as one, they become whole and strong. We need to pull together in order to achieve true success. To reinforce what was demonstrated, the ropes can be pulled out one at a time to reiterate the fact that the groups, though appearing equal, are still three different types.

Part 2 • Games

Organized play that includes competition on an individual or team basis. They can be related to an educational objective or be used as a team building tool.

Equal Distant Game

History: This is another activity that comes from my leadership camp experiences. The camp program in Wisconsin is divided into week long segments and one of the chief objectives at all levels is team building. This activity shows how the actions of one person can affect others.

Materials: None

Time: 10 -15 minutes

Group Size: Any number

Description: This is a group activity. The group you will be working with should number at least 8-10 and can be much larger if you desire. The great feature of the activity is that it can be done with large groups. Instruct the group that they are to pick out two people in the room. They should not let anyone know whom they have chosen. When you (the facilitator) signal the start of the activity, every person must move around the room trying to keep their two people an equal distance away from themselves. This process should continue until it seems like the group has ceased moving. If they stop moving, they have most likely reached a state of congruence.

When the group reaches this state, ask one of the participants to move to another section of the room or you might instruct them to leave the room altogether. Allow a short period of time to see how this new movement affects the group and stop the exercise. Bring the group back together and process the activity.

Learning Connections:

I would suggest that you use questions from the following list when you process:

1. How did you pick out the two people in whom you were keeping an equal distance?
2. Could you tell if you had been chosen by anyone?
3. What was the feeling as the group moved to accomplish the task?
4. Why did the group's movements seem to slow down?
5. How was the group affected when we asked one person to move?
6. How can we compare the results of this activity to what happens in real life group situations?
7. How could our performance have been improved if we were able to communicate?

It is important to highlight the concept of how everyone in a group has a big role to play no matter what their position is. Good groups, teams, or classes value everyone and appreciate the fact that everyone can have a positive impact if they feel valued.

Mystic Writing

History: This activity comes from past camp and summer recreation sources.

Materials: The only material needed is a long straight object (broom, bat, golf club, etc.). However, when you do the activity, you must be working with another person who understands the system. The game is a form of communication between you and the other person. The object of the game is for the group members to figure out how the information is being transmitted between the facilitator and the chosen person.

Time: 20 - 30 minutes

Group Size: Any number

Description: To begin, have the selected person turn his or her back or leave the room while the group comes up with a word. The word can be a person, place or thing. Bring back the helper after the word has been chosen.

Now the process of mystic writing begins. The writer takes a long straight object and begins to move it randomly around the floor. For purposes of demonstration, I will use the word "PACKERS," as in the Green Bay Packers of the NFL. What I want to do, as the mystic writer, is spell out a clue to the chosen word. The signals to answer are as follows:

1. A **clap** starts the exercise and signals the end of a word or clue.

2. Consonants are derived from spoken phrases.

3. Vowels are given by taping the writing object on the ground.

Back to PACKERS, there are several ways to signal this. If you want to simply spell it out you would do the following:

1. **Clap** starts the clue.

2. Give a phrase like, "**P**lease watch what I am doing."

The word "please" starts the phrase and gives the first consonant. Please starts with **P,** hence you have the first letter in **P**ackers. The first letter in the first word of the phrase is the signal for all consonants.

4. After you say the phrase, start tracing the ground with the stick. This means nothing for the clue. It is just done to throw off the group.

5. Next we would need an **A** for the second letter in P**A**CKERS. **A** is a vowel; vowels are signaled by taping the writing stick on the floor. One tap for "A," two taps for "E," three taps for "I," four taps for "O" and five taps for "U."

After one tap for the **A** in PACKERS, begin randomly drawing on the floor again. In order to finish the word, you could proceed as follows:

*Say, "**C**an you see what is happening?"

Draw – draw – draw – draw

*Say, "**K**eep your eyes open."

Draw – draw – draw – draw

*Tap two times for **E.**

Draw – draw – draw – draw

*Say, "**R**emember to watch what I am doing."

Draw – draw – draw – draw

*Say, "**S**ee the answer."

Clap (to signify the end of the clue).

It is best if you do not always just spell out the word. It adds to the game if you use clues instead. An example clue for Packers might be something like "NFL G BAY."

Learning Connections: It is a great activity for free time when you want to occupy a small group. As you do this activity, the observers will begin to figure it out. Once they have solved it, they will have a connection with you as you both share the answer.

Ping Pong Ball Flick

History: This is a game I learned at Leadership Camp. It is one of a series of active games used to team build and bond called "Junior Olympics." The object of Junior Olympics is to use fun and competition to aide in team building. This  particular activity is one of my favorites, as it looks very easy, but in fact it is very difficult.

Materials: You will need a number of ping-pong balls and one plastic soda bottle. It may be necessary to secure the bottle with tape to the surface on which it is sitting. The ping-pong balls are placed on the mouth of the bottle. The bottle should be waist level above the floor. The participants will need room to attempt to flick off the ball while they are walking by it. It also helps to have an additional leader or student volunteer to chase and retrieve the ping-pong balls.

Time: 5 - 10 minutes

Group Size: 10 - 15 people per group

Description: The group should be lined up 15 to 20 feet away from the secured bottle. The facilitator stands by the bottle and is in a position to replace the ball if it is knocked off. The facilitator also acts as a judge and scorekeeper.

The rules are as follows:

1. The participants take turns trying to flick the ball off the bottle. Each person must complete his or her attempt before the next attempt is made.

2. In making an attempt, the participants must walk continually and not slow down or stop.

3. Their arms must be straight and they must use their index fingers to flick at the ball.

4. They are not allowed to hit the bottle.

5. If they knock the ball off, they must pick it up and return it to the facilitator.

6. Their team gets one point for each ball knocked off.

Learning Connections: This is another example of what looks to be an easy task that can be difficult. It is fun and good for team building. Processing questions could be directed to topics like:

1. Practice makes us better.

2. Learn from our mistakes.

3. Slow down for success.

4. Everybody makes mistakes.

Polar Bears Around the Ice Hole

History: This game has a long history. I found it in an old math book and also in a scout camp manual. It is basically a game built around a riddle. Once the riddle is figured out, playing the game is easy. During the game, participants tend to look too deeply into trying to solve it.

Materials: A set of five regular dice. To make it more fun, I also provide award buttons for those who figure out the game. An official *Polar Bear Playing Set* can be purchased. See www.energizerolson.com for ordering information.

Time: 5 - 10 minutes each time you do it

Group Size: Any number

Description: The game is to make Polar Bears out of the participants. They can become Polar Bears if they are able to correctly determine the number of Polar Bears that appear when the dice are rolled. Before the dice are rolled, the following riddle is said. The solution to the game is secretly stated in the riddle. The riddle goes as follows:

> *The game is in the name*
> *As in the days of Gengis Kahn*
> *Like polar bears around an ice hole*
> *Or pedals around a rose*
> *How many polar bears*
> *Do you see?*

At this point, roll the dice and allow the group members to guess or figure out the solution. After they have all guessed, give them the correct answer. Continue this process of saying the riddle, rolling the dice and guessing the number of Polar Bears until someone in the group understands the riddle. In order to become an official Polar Bear, a person has to get the correct answer three times in succession.

The solution is quite simple. The only dice that contain Polar Bears are those that have a dot in the middle (an ice hole). The dots around the middle dot are considered the Polar Bears. For example, each number three die has 2 Polar Bears and each number 5 die has four Polar Bears.

When someone figures out the riddle, swear them into the Polar Bear Society. Have them raise their right hand and say the following oath:

I, _____
Solemnly swear that I
Will not reveal the secret
Of the great game
Knowing full well that
If I do, I will betray
The great Polar Bear society.

At this point, I present the new member with an official Polar Bear pin. (See the resources section for information on the availability of Polar Bear pins.) The whole activity is fun and it engages the group.

Learning Connections: When I work with a group for a longer period of time (a week-long camp or a day-long workshop), I like to present it early and have group members use it during breaks, meals and any other down times.

Breaking Away

History: I first saw this done over 25 years ago at a national adult leadership conference. It is a basic problem-solving situation that is difficult to figure out at first, because people will not think outside the box. It allows you to teach many different concepts related to the process people go through in solving problems.

Materials: One connection string is needed for each participant. These can be easily made from yarn or any medium strength string. (A loop is tied in each end. The loop should be big enough to fit over the participants' wrists.)

Time: 20 - 30 minutes

Group Size: Any number

Description: I like to begin this activity by having one or two pairs of people try the trick while the rest of the group observes. The pairs are to be connected together. The object is to have the pairs get unconnected. In the process they are *not allowed* to do any of the following:

1. Break the strings.
2. Untie the strings.
3. Take the strings off their wrists.

As the chosen pair struggles with the problem, I make myself available to answer questions. In most cases, the pairs will go ahead and try what they think will work. After a time, they will become discouraged and frustrated.

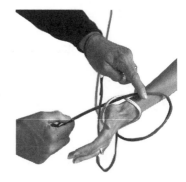

At this point, I intervene and show the group the correct method.

In order to solve the problem one person must hold their arms out, stretching their string straight out. Their partner will do

the trick by finding the space near one of the wrists. This space created by the knot. The trick will work using the space near either wrist.

To complete the activity the person doing the trick brings their string up to the space, reaches in and pulls their string through the space. This loop of string is put over the partners hand. After putting it over the hand, let it go and have the person pull their arms apart.

At this point the two people will no longer be tied together.

I challenge those who have figured it out to make everyone successful by helping others. I have had groups as large as 600 solve this problem in three minutes, which is only possible if the group helps one another. It is fun to finish the activity by having the total group test their abilities under pressure. I have them get set up and decide who will do the trick first. I give a starting signal and have them indicate their completion by raising their hands.

Learning Connections: I use this activity to teach about study skills in my guidance classes. In order to find the answer to the problem, the group needs to ask questions. I relate this fact to the need to ask questions in school and all learning situations. When good questions are asked and correct information is given, problems can be solved. In addition, the idea of working together and how it contributes to group success can be emphasized.

I have a friend who is a health educator. She uses this activity to teach about relationships in her marriage and family classes. It highlights the concept of getting stuck in a bad relationship and how to work out of it.

Surfer Wave Girl

History: I picked up this activity from a friend named Patty Hupfer Reidel. Patty and I worked together at a leadership camp for many summers. It was always great to get together as we would exchange ideas and activities. This is one activity she showed me. I have made great use of it ever since. Patty is an activities director for a school in Milwaukee. Contact information for Patty can be found in the resources section.

Materials: None

Time: 5 - 10 minutes

Group Size: Any number

Description: This is a game like "Rock, Paper, Scissors." It can be played with pairs of people or in small groups. The object is to beat your partner(s). I use it to open up discussion about competition. There are three actions used in the game. They are:

1. **Surfer**

2. **Wave**

3. **Girl**

The game is played by having the partner(s) standing back to back. On the command of the facilitator, the participants turn around, face their partner(s) and do one of the actions. Participants can score points in the following way.

> If I do the **Surfer** and my partner does **Wave**,
I get a point as the **Surfer** gets the **Wave**.

Surfer

> If I do **Wave** and my partner does **Girl**,
I get a point as the **Wave** gets the **Girl**.

> If I do **Girl** and my partner does **Surfer**,
I get a point as the **Girl** gets the **Surfer**.

I play the game for a set number of times. Four to five times works well for me. In all cases, the group will have fun and it is a good transition or introduction activity.

Wave

Girl

Learning Connections: Competition is a double-edged sword in our everyday life. On one hand, competition can make all of us better by causing improved performance. The problem we face is the level of discourse and feelings that take place when competition is only seen as a win/lose situation. It is healthy to compete, but the value that is taken from good win/win competition is something we should promote in education.

Wave

I try to process activities like this to show competition can be fun and all parties can get something out of it. In this activity, all participants try to win, have fun and build relationships at the same time.

When Someone Claps Twice

History: My family has a long history with 4-H. All of my children were involved. The 4-H agents and staff members have vast backgrounds from which to draw upon in their work. I have learned a great deal from these people, and I have been able to apply the ideas to my work. One of my best friends in 4-H is an agent from Minnesota named Anne Stevenson. Anne gave me this activity while she and I were working together at a summer leadership camp.

Materials: You need a copy of the attached worksheet cut into pieces so there is one saying on each slip of paper. Each participant receives one of the sayings. There are 27 parts to the activity. If your group has less than 27 people, you can give additional sheets to selected participants. If there are more than 27 people, you can include slips that say, "Do nothing." Lastly, you will need enough candy to be able to give a piece to everyone.

Time: 15 - 30 minutes

Group Size: Any number

Description: Have a discussion about the importance of everyone doing their part in a group. Stress the point that complex tasks often require an order or sequence to be successful. Tell the group we all have to do our part and there are no shortcuts to success. In this activity, each person will have a job to do and they will have to be ready to do their job at the correct time.

Pass out the slips of paper and have the participants read their jobs. Let them know you have a job to do, as well, and you will do it. After everyone has read their slip and you have their attention, start the game by clapping twice. The participants are to follow as their job comes up. There will be confusion and the system may break down or go out of order. When this happens, stop the game, recognize the mistake, encourage the group and start again by clapping twice.

Learning Connections: Processing Questions

1. Did everyone understand the directions that were given?
2. What did you think when you read your job slip?
3. What caused the efforts to break down?
4. Why was it easier each time after we had to start over?
5. What did we have to do in order to be successful?
6. How important was each person to the success of the group?
7. How does this activity relate to the concepts of:
   a. Everyone must contribute in order to have success?
   b. Everyone has an important role to play?

When someone claps twice, stand up and say, "Good Morning."	*When someone says, "I'm glad to be here," whistle.*
When someone says, "Good Morning," get up and turn off the lights.	*When someone whistles, stand up and flap your arms like a bird.*
When someone turns off the lights, clap once and yell, "It's dark in here."	*When someone flaps their arms like a bird, stand on your chair.*
When someone yells, "It's dark in here," get up and turn on the lights.	*When someone stands on their chair, say, "Get down from there."*
When someone turns on the lights, stand up and spin around twice.	*When someone says, "Get down from there," make a loud sneezing sound.*
When someone spins around twice, make a cow noise.	*When someone makes a loud sneezing sound, feel the forehead of the person next to you and shout, "Someone get a doctor."*
When someone makes a cow noise, stand up and say, "I'm glad to be here."	*When someone shouts, "Someone get a doctor," sing, "I'm a Little Teapot."*

When someone sings, *"I'm a Little Teapot,"* walk around the group leader three times.	When someone says, *"I have a question,"* say, *"I have an answer."*
When someone walks around the group leader three times, laugh really loud.	When someone says, *"I have an answer,"* come to the front and make the letter Y with your arms.
When someone laughs really loud, stomp your feet.	When someone makes a Y with their arms, choose two other people, come to the front and make the letters M, C, and A.
When someone stomps their feet, do a cheerleading move or jump.	When someone makes the letters M, C, and A, hop on one foot for five seconds.
When someone does a cheerleading move or jump, tell us what time it is.	When someone hops on one foot, say, *"Here comes Peter Cottontail."*
When someone tells us what time it is, shake hands and introduce yourself to the tallest male in the room.	When someone says, *"Here comes Peter Cottontail,"* give everyone a piece of candy.
When someone introduces themselves to the tallest male in the room, say, *"I have a question."*	Do nothing.

Captain is Coming

History: This is a group activity that I believe came to me from my experiences with 4-H. My children were active in 4-H and I have found 4-H and University Extension to be valuable resources for ideas that work with groups. This is an elimination game similar to Simon Says.

Materials: None. The activity only requires an open space large enough to accommodate a group. For this activity to be successful, I would suggest a group size of 12 or more.

Time: 15 - 20 minutes

Group Size: Any number

Description: To begin, the group should spread out in the workspace. I like to have boundaries established for all group members active in the game. The space where the game is played is supposed to be the deck of a ship. The front of the boat is where the leader stands. The game has the following commands:

1. **CAPTAIN IS COMING:** When the leader gives this command, all the group members must face the leader and stand at attention. From this point, no one is allowed to move unless the command of AT EASE is given.

2. **AT EASE:** This command releases the group to move for other commands. If anyone moves without the command of AT EASE, they are out of the game.

Carl Olson

3. **BOW:** On this command, the group members must face in the direction of the leader (bow of the boat). If they face the wrong way, they are out of the game.

4. **STERN:** On this command, the group members must face the back of the boat away from the leader. If they face the wrong way, they are out of the game.

5. **PORT:** On this command, the group members must face to the port or left side of the boat. If they face the wrong way, they are out of the game.

6. **STARBOARD:** On this command, the group members must face to the starboard or right side of the boat. Again, if they face the wrong way, they are out of the game.

7. **MAN OVER BOARD**: On this command, each group member must find a partner and have one person crouch down and yell for help. The other person comes to their rescue, offers a hand, and helps them up. If a group member does not find a partner, they are out of the game.

8. **SEA SICK:** When this command is heard, the group members must pretend to be throwing up.

9. **CAPTAINS BALL:** This command requires each group member to find a partner and dance. If a

group member does not find a partner, they are out of the game.

10. **ROW BOAT:** On this command, group members must get into groups of three. They then sit on the floor and pretend to be rowing a boat. If any group members are not a part of a group of three, they are out of the game.

The leader explains the calls before the game begins and proceeds to call out the commands throughout the game. The group members attempt to perform the instructed directions. Remember that a CAPTAIN IS COMING command should freeze the group until and AT EASE command is given. The leader can try to throw off the group members by calling commands after saying CAPTAIN IS COMING. If at any time the group members make a mistake, do the wrong action, or do not find the necessary partner or partners, they are out of the game. Play is continued until a predetermined number of people remain. I have the players who are eliminated act as judges as the game continues.

Learning Connections: Students of all ages find this to be an enjoyable activity. I also have used it as a class competition by having an equal number of students from each class play the game. The object is to have most classmates remaining in the game at the end of the game.

Banana Bandana?

History: This is a skit that I use to get across the idea of clear communications. It works very well for school groups, but I would not be afraid to use it for adult groups, as well. The activity is fun with a solid message. It gets across the idea that the communications process is complex and easily confused.

Materials: One or more willing volunteers whom you have prepared ahead of time. Each volunteer needs to have a banana and a yellow bandanna.

Procedure: Start out the presentation by saying you are a magician and you will be demonstrating a new trick today as part of the program. Call forth your trained volunteers and have them stand behind you so you cannot see them.

Time: 15 - 20 minutes

Group Size: Any number

Next, note that your volunteers will be working with one of two objects. The two objects are a banana and a bandanna. Start the directions by asking the volunteers if they can hear you. Next tell them to drop the banana. Say it fast so they can act confused. Repeat it again and in the confusion they will set down the opposite object or the bandanna.

The directions continue as follows:

1. Open the bandanna.
2. Fold it in half.
3. Fold it again.
4. Make it disappear.
5. Make it reappear.

   The volunteers will play along with you and seem confused. The fun part comes when you ask them to make it disappear. At this point, they will put it in their mouth. Then when asked to make it reappear, they spit it into their hands and this causes a reaction from the group, at which time you look back and the volunteers exit.

   It is great fun and you can make points about the importance of good communications and asking questions.

Learning Connections: The point of this skit is to show how confusing communications can really be. We have all played the telephone game and know how the message can be changed as it is passed from one person to the next. This is a visible large group way of showing this. Following up this activity allows you to discuss the importance of asking questions to clarify what needs to be done.

Field Goal

History: We can learn from anyone, anywhere. I picked this up at an elementary leadership conference. A sixth grade student took me up on my offer to share and learn new ideas. He came up to me after my presentation and gave me this quick, thought-provoking activity.

Materials: You need four straight objects and one small round one. Some suggestions for the straight pieces could be toothpicks, straws or popsicle sticks. The small round object can be a coin or something of similar size. I like this activity because it can be carried in your pocket and it can be done with one person, a small group, a class or a large audience. When working with a large group, I would suggest putting the objects on an overhead projector.

Description: Setup the objects as pictured. The goal of the activity is to get the round object outside of the enclosed area by only moving two of 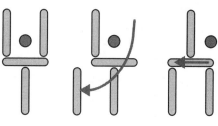 the straight objects. After the objects are moved, the field goal shape should be retained, with the round object no longer inside the shape.

Learning Connections: Using creative mental challenges, is an excellent way to open dialog and build teams. Having an individual work on this first, then moving to small groups will allow different perspectives to come into play. It is an excellent example of how difficult simple tasks can be.

King Frog

History: In 1996, I had the chance to attend a training course through Project Adventure. The course I took was called *Adventure Based Counseling.* It was an informative learning experience. In the evening, our group would get together to socialize. One evening, a group member introduced us to the game, King Frog. This game provided us hours of fun and entertainment.

Materials: You need to create an animal for each member of the group. I suggest putting the names of the animals on cards and placing the cards under the chairs where the participants are sitting.

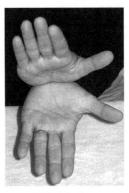

Alligator

Description: This activity works best with groups of 20 or under. Seat the group in a circle and pass out the animal cards. Put a card under each chair and the person sitting in that chair becomes that animal for the game. Create an action for each animal *(See examples).* The King Frog sits in position 1 and the goal of all of the players is to become the King Frog. The King Frog starts the game. The action of the King Frog is done by slapping one hand over the other and saying, "King Frog."

Elephant

After the King Frog says and does their action, they follow it by saying and doing the action of another animal. The person who is the animal invoked by the King Frog

Moose

must keep the activity going by saying and doing their name and action and then the name and action of another animal. They can say and do any action including the King Frog.

The object of the game is to get the people ahead of you to make a mistake. If anyone fails to respond when their animal is called, the game is stopped and that person moves to last place in the circle and everyone moves up to fill their place. Also, if anyone says the wrong thing or makes the wrong action, the same consequence occurs. Each time a mistake is made, the person who is the King Frog gets a point. Continue playing as long as you want and try to find who can be the greatest King Frog.

NFL Teams

History: This activity was part of a leadership junior Olympics with which I assisted. Junior Olympics activities are designed to team build and use a wide variety of skills and talents. In doing so, we tried to find areas of expertise where all involved could contribute. This mental activity tests the group's knowledge of sports.

Materials: Have one copy of the NFL Teams Worksheet for each group member. Distribute the answer sheet after the activity. Use this to correct and score the groups results.

Time: 15 - 20 minutes

Group Size: Any number

Description: You can do this in a variety of ways. Have students work on it individually or put them in teams. Give them a set time period. I would suggest ten to twelve minutes to get as many answers correct as possible. Score the results and honor the winning team. If I am working with students, I like to encourage them to take a copy of the activity home and make it a family activity. I have them report back the next day. It helps me learn something about their home. Who did they do it with? How well did their home group score? Asking questions like these gives me insight into their families.

NFL Teams Answers

1. Giants	2. 49ers
3. Patriots	4. Bears
5. Jets	6. Raiders
7. Steelers	8. Browns
9. Bills	10. Packers
11. Dolphins	12. Falcons
13. Texans	14. Vikings
15. Rams	16. Eagles
17. Cowboys	18. Cardinals
19. Chiefs	20. Chargers
21. Bengals	22. Buccaneers
23. Red Skins	24. Seahawks
25. Saints	26. Broncos
27. Colts	28. Lions
29. Jaguars	30. Panthers
31. Titans	32. Ravens

NFL Teams Worksheet

There are 32 NFL teams. Identify each team represented by the description of their mascot.

1. Army Insect   1. _____
2. Seven Squared   2. _____
3. Fighter for Country   3. _____
4. Streakers are This   4. _____
5. A 747   5. _____
6. Hostile Attackers   6. _____
7. Thieves   7. _____
8. Sun Tanned Bodies   8. _____
9. Invoices   9. _____
10. Helpers to Relocate   10. _____
11. Miniature Scuba Gear   11. _____
12. Bird Trained to Kill   12. _____
13. Lone Star   13. _____
14. Six Rulers   14. _____
15. Opposite of Ewe   15. _____
16. Class of Boy Scouts   16. _____
17. American Gauchos   17. _____
18. Fundamental Rule   18. _____
19. Indian Leader   19. _____
20. Credit Card Users   20. _____
21. Used to Be Girls   21. _____
22. A Dollar for Corn   22. _____
23. Hot Epidermis   23. _____
24. View of the Predator   24. _____
25. Louis Armstrong Favorite   25. _____
26. Rodeo Horses   26. _____
27. Six Shooters   27. _____
28. King of the Beasts   28. _____
29. Expensive Car   29. _____
30. Black Cats   30. _____
31. Another Large Warrior   31. _____
32. Edgar Allen Poe Bird   32. _____

Carl Olson

Balloon Problem Solving Activity

Materials: The participants are divided into groups of 10-20. Each group needs a facilitator. The group works with the following materials: 100 small multicolored balloons, 100 pieces of string, 1 large garbage bag, and 1 pin.

Time: 25-40 minutes

Group Size: 10-20

Rules: The leader holds the bag. The participants try pass or give the balloons to the leader. The leader will only accept the balloon if it meets the following criteria:

1. Balloons must be filled to at least 50% capacity.
2. A string must be tied to each balloon.
3. Balloons must be passed with the left hand.
4. Do not accept consecutive balloons of the same color.
   All balloons that do not meet the criteria will be popped by the leader

Learning Connections: Teamwork and observation are necessary to solve the problem. Teams that are successful will take suggestions from all the people in the group. Some teams never solve the problem, nearly all will get some balloons in just by chance. Have the team review how they went about solving the problem and make suggestions to improve in future activities. Comparisons should be made to real life situations.

Cup Stack

Materials: You will need 10 plastic cups and a rubber band for each group of six participants. Tie a six-foot piece of string for each participant to the rubber band as shown in the picture.

Description: The object of the activity is to stack the cups into a pyramid as a group. This list of rules must be followed:

1. Only the rubber band with the strings tied to it may be used to stack the cups.

2. All participants must hold the free end of strings. This allows the group to move and stretch the rubber band around the cups.

3. In the beginning of the activity, the students will be allowed to talk. At some point during the activity, however, the facilitator will announce that talking is no longer allowed.

4. This is a timed activity. The group that creates the pyramid in the fastest time is the winner.

    When setting up the activity, spread out the cups: some mouth up, mouth down or some on their sides. Use the same combination for each group.

Learning Connections:

1. What strategies did you try to pick up the cups? Which worked? Why? Which did not work? Why not?

2. How did being allowed to talk or not talk affect your cooperative work?

3. Did any leaders emerge? How did this affect the group?

Carl Olson

Part 3 • Initiatives

Activities that go beyond games and energizers. They are exploratory in nature creating more in-depth analysis of thoughts, feelings, impressions, and reactions. In order for them to be effective, they must always be followed with processing questions.

Sticks 'N Stones

History: I first saw this activity at a National Association of Workshop Directors (N.A.W.D.) meeting in Seattle. It came from a fellow camp director named Connie Miley. Connie is from Ohio, and she developed this activity as a closing piece for a camp session.

Materials: For this activity you would need the following:

1. 1 ziplock sandwich bag

2. 3 sharp round pencils

3. Enough water to fill the bag ½ full

4. 2 spoonfuls of sodium polyacrylate *"Slush Powder."* It is a super adsorbent polymer that can be obtained from various sources. *Slush Powder* is included in the *Impact Pak*.

5. 1 lighter or book of matches

6. A piece of flash cotton.
See www.energizerolson.com for ordering information.

Time: 10 - 20 minutes.

Group Size: It will work for any size group.

Description: I use the activity to demonstrate the concepts of self-esteem or success. I start by presenting the bag with the water in it. I make the point that we all have a certain amount of

---

self-esteem. I have the water represent their self-esteem. They can add to it in any number of ways (join a club, do good works, play a sport and so on).

Next, I point out they can detract from their self-esteem in the following three ways. Using the three pencils one at a time, I punch them through the bag of water as I explain the three detractors. The water will not leak as the plastic forms around the pencil. The pencils represent:

1. **You:** We all put ourselves down and always look at what is wrong with us. In doing so, we take a shot at our self-esteem, just like the pencil is going through the bag.

2. **Other People:** People say things to us to put us down or discourage us. This also detracts from the level of confidence we would like to have.

3. **Life Circumstances:** Bad things happen to everyone. You have an argument with your best friend; you get a poor grade on an assignment and so on. Once again, these circumstances take a shot at your self-esteem.

You now have three pencils punched through the bag. These three objects represent the point that has been made. In the next phase, you make the point that in order to cope with these pressures, we need to make changes. At this time, put the slush powder into the bag of water. The powder will turn the water to a solid. Then, one by one, pull the pencils out of the bag and explain how to deal with each situation.

1. **You:** When we look at you, we just see your positives. If you look at yourself in the same way, you will be able to keep your self-esteem in tack.

2. **Other People:** If your friends, or the people you find yourself in the company of, are not a positive influence, try to find people who are positive. Do not let other people hold you back. In your dealings with people, try to model positive behavior. This will set a tone for the development of strong supportive relationships.

3. **Circumstances:** Good and bad things happen to people everyday. How you adjust to and handle these situations makes all the difference. Find people to talk to that will listen and offer help. Developing your faith and a positive attitude also will help you through the ups and downs of life.

After this part of the demonstration, take out a small amount of the flash cotton and a lighter.

Explain that everyone has a bad day. Compare the cotton to a bad day. Note that bad days can be dealt with if they are kept under control. Say bad days can be controlled, just like you can mold or shape the cotton.

At this point use the lighter to light the cotton. This will cause a flash and a puff of smoke. Make the point that bad days or low feelings can be nothing but smoke if we handle them correctly.

Processing Questions:

1. What does the bag of water represent?

2. Give some examples of ways to add to your self-esteem.

3. The pencils were examples of ways your self-esteem can be attacked. What did each pencil represent?

4. Adding the slush powder changed the water. How can you change your lives to help with the three problems presented?

5. The flash cotton represented bad days we all can have. When do bad days happen and what causes them?

6. What suggestions can you list to help you to handle bad days?

Who Spoiled the Fun?

History: This activity was given to me at a regional counselor conference in Abilene, Texas. There were school counselors and clinical counselors in attendance. A clinical counselor named Russ Saunders shared this activity with me. He used it as an educational tool for teaching about STDs (sexually transmitted diseases).

Materials: A package of regular Oreo cookies and a container in which to put them. The container should have a top on it so you can mix up the cookies.

Time: 12 - 20 minutes

Group Size: Any number

Description: The activity is very simple, based on the fact almost everyone likes Oreo cookies. That feeling can be used as a metaphor to compare Oreos to the teaching point you are making. An example would be friendship. You begin by having a discussion about friendship, the importance of good friends, and all the positives involved in true friend- centered relationships. Next, open up the container of Oreo cookies and ask the group if they recognize them. Now, compare their knowledge of Oreo cookies to the concepts of friendship previously discussed.

The discussion should then switch to the ways people break down and destroy friendships. Examples would be breaking a trust, being dishonest, or even taking friendships for

---

granted. Take out one of the Oreos, break it open, lick the inside of it and put it back together. Then put the Oreo back in the container, replace the cover, and mix them up. Now open the container and offer the cookies to the group. No matter how much they like Oreos, they will be very reluctant to try them because they do not know which one you have licked.

Learning Connections: In this case, I used the activity to make a comparison between the licked Oreo and the effects of our actions on the dynamics of friendship. Licking the Oreo and putting it back in the container changes everyone's feelings. Likewise, dishonesty, unfaithfulness or other negative actions have profound effects on friendship.

Lighter Than Air

History: I was introduced to this activity while presenting at the Wisconsin State Teachers Convention. While on a break between presentations, I sat in on a session in the room next to mine. It was put on by John Irvin, a facilitator trainer from Oklahoma. The resources section has information about John Irvin and his work. I took the "Lighter Than Air" activity from this session and I have used it as a warm-up for groups. It takes team effort and concentration in order to accomplish the objective of the activity.

Materials: This activity can be done with a variety of materials. For small groups of five or less, a hula-hoop will work. For larger groups  of six to fifteen, a fiber tent pole has been my choice of equipment. Tent poles are good because they come in sections and you can add enough sections to accommodate the size of the group.

Time: 5 - 10 minutes

Group Size: 4 - 6 per hula hoop, 15-20 per tent pole

Description: Begin the activity by having group members hold the object at eye level by resting the tip of one index finger underneath it. At the signal of the facilitator, the group must lower the object to knee level. They are not allowed to grab it, and they all must be in contact with it at all times.

This seems like an easy task, but when the facilitator lets go, the group will force the object up in the air instead of down. This reaction happens because they are all supporting the object. In doing this, they are applying upward pressure. Every time someone loses contact with the object, the facilitator should start the activity over again from the original starting position. After several trials, the group will get the correct feel for the activity. In order to solve it, they must work together as a group and concentrate.

Learning Connections: Teamwork is the essence of this activity. The group will experience frustration and disbelief at first. Good processing questions for this activity would be:

1. Did everyone understand the directions?
2. Did this seem like it was going to be a difficult task?
3. How did it feel on the first several trials?
4. Why was the task so difficult?
5. What did the group need to do to move toward success?
6. How is this process like similar tasks we face in life?

Snow Flake

History: This is an exercise in following and interrupting directions. I like it because it is an example of active learning. It is a visual example of how difficult verbal communication really is. I have seen this used by many trainers, and it never fails to make the point.

Materials: Each participant will need an 8½ inch by 11 inch sheet of paper. It can be lined or unlined. They will be tearing the paper, so it is always a good idea to have enough wastebaskets available.

Time: 15 - 20 minutes

Group Size: Any number

Description: When each person has their sheet of paper, give the following directions:

1. Fold the paper in half.
2. Fold it in half again.
3. Tear off the upper right-hand corner.
4. Tear off a piece from the middle of the bottom side.
5. Fold the paper into a triangle.
6. Tear off two of the corners of the triangle.
7. Tear off a piece from the middle of the bottom side of the triangle.
8. Now unfold the paper and compare your snowflake to the other people in the group.

Carl Olson

Give the direction clearly, but do not answer questions. You may change the directions as you wish, but the object of the activity is to have the participants try to interpret your directions. In the end, everyone in the group will have heard the same directions, but they will come up with different solutions, based on their understanding of the directions.

Just as there are no two real snowflakes are alike, all of the participants' snowflakes will be different. Each person decodes or understands the directions differently.

Look Beyond

History: I learned this group activity in college. It was used as a party game. Since that time, I have seen it in books and many other settings. A few years back, I attended Project Adventure training and they described how this game is used with their youth program.

Materials: Ten like objects are used to make patterns. The objects can be anything: sticks, paper clips, tooth picks, or whatever is handy and can be seen by the group in which you are working. With larger groups, the objects can be placed on an overhead projector. In addition to the objects, a pad of paper and something to write with will be needed.

Time: 15 - 20 minutes

Group Size: Class room size group (20-30)

Description: This is another activity where you are working with a preselected assistant. The assistants  need to be prepared ahead of time so they can be in on the trick to the activity. Explain to the group you have developed a system of communicating numbers by making patterns with the objects. The system allows you to show the numbers from zero to ten. Pick out a person from the group (your preselected helper) and have the group observe while you set up your first pattern. While they are looking at it, write the number on a piece of paper. Finally, have the helper reveal an interpretation of the pattern. After this is done, show the group that you and your assistant got the same answer.

The trick to the activity is the secret communication between you and the helper. You use talking and elaborate patterns to involve the group, but the correct answer is not in the objects nor is it in what you say. It lies instead in your hand signals. After you make the patterns, simply use your fingers to give the answer. Closed fists represent zero, while the other numbers are represented through the number of fingers you display.

Learning Connections: This activity works well as an interesting and fun game, but I also have found it useful as a teaching tool. When people first attempt to figure out the solution to this activity, they concentrate on the objects and look for patterns. In fact, in order to solve it, they have to look beyond the objects to see the real solution. Many times, in group situations, we need to look beyond what is obvious to get to the real problem.

Pipeline

History: I first learned this at a team-building training I attend for my school. Since that time, I have seen it in various other sources. I like the activity because it is simple, yet it challenges group members to think creatively.

Materials: Each participant will need a piece of PCV pipe split open in half. I use pipe pieces that are one and one half feet long and I cut them from 1½ inch PCV pipe. These items are easily made.

In addition to the pipe, you will need objects to roll down the pipeline. I use golf balls and marbles. The golf balls work best with 1½ inch PCV pipe and the marbles will work with any size pipe. You also will need a receptacle of some type to act as a deposit site for your objects. I recommend a coffee can or small wastebasket.

Time: 10 minutes practice/planning,

20 - 25 minutes for activity trial

Group Size: 15 - 20

Description: Show the objects used in the activity to the group. Set up the problem by establishing a start point and a goal some distance away. The goal is the receptacle. I have it at least 75 feet away. The more participants, the greater the distance between the start line and the goal.

Give the following rules:

1. They need to move as many of the objects from the start line to the goal in 20 minutes.

2. The objects must roll down the pieces of PCV pipe.

3. The objects must always roll forward once they start moving. They cannot stop moving or roll backwards. If either of these things happens, the object must be started over.

4. Persons holding the PCV pipe when the objects are on it must not move their feet. Participants are allowed to move when they do not have an object on their piece of pipe.

5. Participants are not allowed to touch the objects with their hands.

6. Participants are not allowed to touch their pipe piece with any of the other participants' pipe pieces. The object must be passed from person to person without contacting pipe pieces.

Give the group up to ten minutes to practice. Ask them to set a goal for their twenty-minute trial. After the trial period and goal setting, begin the exercise. During the twenty-minute period, act as a referee. Answer questions based on the rules laid out in the beginning.

Processing Questions:

1. Did your group make good use of your planning time?

2. How did you come up with your goal?

3. Was your goal realistic?

4. Did your group make changes in your method?

5. What prompted the changes you made?

6. Was it better to go fast or to take time and be careful?

Sketch Book

History: I first saw this magic trick at a National Workshop Directors conference. See the resources section in the back of this book for availability. I like to use it for children and youth groups.

Materials: All you need is the *Magic Sketchbook* and a large envelope. In the envelope there will be a predetermined picture.
See www.energizerolson.com for ordering information.

Description: I like to start by talking about how police use various face details to come up with a likeness of a person. Show the three parts of the face you can create by flipping through the book. Using the book in this way will show a variety of each of the three areas (heads, noses and chins). There seems to be a vast number of possibilities.

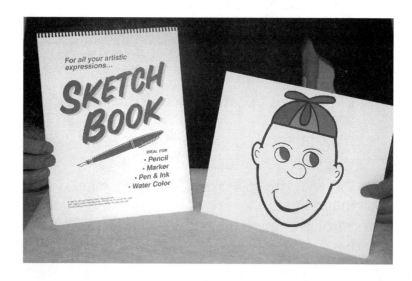

Next, have one of the participants help you create a face. Hold the book off to the side and away from your view and the view of the people who are observing. Ask the chosen helper to tell you when to stop as you randomly flip through the book again. When you have done this with all three areas of the face, show the results. Lastly, have someone open a pre-sealed envelope. In it they will find the exact same face as the one that was just created with the book.

The reason the trick works is every other page is actually a piece of the desired drawing. These pages are cut shorter so when you go through the book in the first direction, it doesn't show them. When the book is turned and paged through in the other direction, only the desired face parts will come up.

Learning Connections: I use this activity to reinforce any of the following concepts:

1. Working together for a desired result.
2. Not leaving anything to chance.
3. The magic of knowledge.

Stress Relief

History: Each year my guidance class is visited by representatives from our area teen runaway shelter. They do a program about their service. In the presentation, they talk about the reasons teens runaway. Troubled teens are under a stress that builds until they feel they have to escape their situation. They use this activity to demonstrate what these stressors are, how they build up and how to deal with them.

Materials: 1. One large laundry basket

2. 20 - 30 large heavy assorted books

Time: 15 - 20 minutes

Group Size: Classroom size group (20 - 30)

Procedure: Begin by discussing stress and the types of situations that bring it on. Ask the group for one volunteer. Have that person stand in front of the group, holding the basket. Ask the group to give examples of stressors they have in their lives. For each  stressor, have them come to the front of the room and take a book from the pile. The books represent their stressors. After they pick them up, have them put them in the basket. It also would be a good idea to write these stressors down on a blackboard or flip chart. The basket will get heavier as more and more stressors are brought up.

After group slows down and has difficulty coming up with more stressors, change the topic to what can be done to relieve stress. Again, ask for examples. As each one is given, have the persons with the suggestions go to the basket and take out one book. When you process the activity, make comparisons to how difficult it is to carry around the stressors in our lives. Review the strategies for handling theses difficult situations.

Learning Connections:

Stress bogs us down. The basket gets heavier with each stressor in our life. What can and should be done? This activity clearly demonstrates this desired concept.

Build a Team

History: This is another activity I learned from my good friend, Anne Stevenson. As I stated earlier, Anne is a University of Minnesota Extension Educator. She is a wealth of information and a great friend. Contact information for Anne can be found in the resources section of this book.

Materials: The following materials are needed:

1. A larger piece of ¼ inch foam core board cut into random size pieces
2. A piece of cardboard or wood to use as a base
3. A set of colored markers
4. A hot glue gun

Time: 15 - 25 minutes

Group Size: 10 - 15 participants

Description: Have each participant select a piece of foam core board. Next, have them design it with information about themselves. Some of the topics you might want them to address in the design could be:

1. A goal they would like to accomplish
2. Family information
3. Interests
4. Values
5. A place they would like to travel
6. A prized possession

After they have finished their piece, have each person come to the front of the group and explain it. Then, have them take the hot glue gun and attach it to the cardboard or wood base. Each person puts their piece where they

want on the board. As the activity proceeds, a sculpture transpires. In the end, we have the information of the individuals connecting together to make a model of the group.

Learning Connection: When we take the time to learn about each other, we increase appreciation. Diversity is more than a race, religion or nationality issue. Generally, we do not take the time to go below the surface to truly understand people. This is a start toward looking differently at the people in our group. It helps to build team spirit and bonding necessary for group success.

Candy X Candy Y

History: I have been very fortunate to have worked with a number of very creative people. A man named Colby Cochran designed this activity. Mr. Cochran is the executive director of the North Carolina Association of School Councils. I have included contact information for him in the resources section of this book. He originally developed this activity for use in his guidance classes and went on to adapt it for leadership groups.

Materials: The following materials are needed to present this activity:

- Candy X Candy Y Worksheets
- Two kinds of candy
  - ◆ **Candy X** is an ugly, green candied peanut. *(See the recipe attached.)*
  - ◆ **Candy Y** is any bright attractive candy. *(It should not have a brand name on it.)*
- Signs with the game information on them. These signs can be hand held, overheads or PowerPoint slides.

Time: 30 - 45 minutes

Group Size: Classroom size group (20 - 30)

Description: This is a simulation activity. Set it up by telling the group they are part of a market survey group. Their task is to test-market two kinds of candy. The results of their survey will help in the purchasing and marketing of the products. When presenting the information, the more realistic and serious you can appear, the better. Inform the group in order to get the best results, they must buy into the

---

activity. The activity proceeds with the following six steps. After each step, the participants will be asked to make their choice. In steps one and two, they are to choose from the two kinds of candy. In steps three through five, they can choose either type of candy or the choice of the **"U"** category for undecided. In the final step six, they still have the three choices, plus the **"N"** category of neither.

1. Start by giving the names of the products.
   Candy X is Venus Supreme
   Candy Y is Passion Delight
   (The sign or slide for Candy X should be plain with black and white print. The sign for Candy Y should be flashy and colorful.)

2. In this step, show the two types of candy to the group.

3. In this step, show the slides of where the candies are made.
   Candy X was made by a seventh grade boy in a F.A.C.E. class.
   Candy Y was made at the Yum Yum Candy Factory.

4. This is the taste test. Note that Candy X was made from peanuts. ***Make sure none of the participants are allergic to peanuts.***

5. In this step, give additional information.
   Candy X: The boy's father is a well-known chef and the boy is an excellent cook.
   Candy Y: The Yum Yum Candy Factory has a sanitation grade of "C," and "things" have been found in the product from time to time.

6. In this final step, give them the chance to say **"N"** for neither.

Learning Connection: The following are the possible processing questions and comments:

1. How many people changed their minds during the course of the activity?
2. What caused you to change your mind?
3. Did everyone come up with the same answer?
4. Is it okay to choose none?
5. How does this compare to the real life decisions we have to make?

The following are points to remember when making decisions:

♦ First decisions might not always be the best ones.

♦ One alternative may have many good points, but one bad point can spoil it.

♦ Everyone did not make the same decision, although everyone heard the same information.

♦ This is a process. If you choose NONE, you have not failed, but only have eliminated two possible options. Pick two more and put them through the same test.

It is okay to be undecided at times.

The following is the recipe for the Candy X.

2 cups	Large red skin peanuts
1 cup	Sugar
½ cup	Water

Green or blue food coloring

Mix all the ingredients together. Bring to a boil and let boil until almost dry

Remove contents and spread on a cookie sheet. Bake at 350 degrees for 10 minutes.

If the nuts begin to burn, remove it earlier.

Candy X Candy Y Worksheet

	X	Y	U	N
1				
2				
3				
4				
5				
6				

Can't Get It Back

History: When I first started teaching, I had a teaching partner in my department who showed me a version of this activity. She used it to teach concepts in her health classes, I adapted it for the topic of gossip.

Materials: A tube of toothpaste for each participant. I would recommend two participants. A roll of paper towels and a box of baby wipes for clean up.

Description: Ask for volunteers that would like a chance to win a prize. I use a $20 bill as a prize, with the knowledge they will not be able to win it.

Step one: Tell the volunteers they have 45 seconds to see how much toothpaste they can squeeze out of the tube. Place a paper towel under their working areas so they do not make a mess on the table. After the time period is over, tell them they can win the $20 by being the first person to get all of the tooth paste back into the tube in two minutes. Encourage the observers to cheer and encourage the participants.

The task is, of course, impossible. Thank and compliment the volunteers and have a consolation prize for them. I use some kind of candy I know they would like.

Time: 10 - 15 minutes

Group Size: Any number of participants

Learning Connection: Processing questions:

1. How many of you were willing to volunteer for the activity in the beginning?
2. Was this a fair contest?
3. How did the volunteers try to accomplish the task?
4. How is this activity like gossip?

   • People willing to participate in it without considering the consequences.

   • Once gossip is out, we can not get it back.

   • The clean up or follow up to gossip is a mess, just like the tooth paste.

   • We would all be better off if we checked information out and did not misuse it. Toothpaste is not for play. When used correctly, it has a positive effect on us.

Newspaper Fashion Show

Materials: Each group will be provided with a stack of newspapers, approximately one foot to two feet high. They also are provided with a roll of masking tape.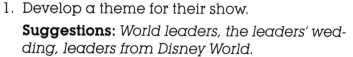

Time: 20-30 minutes

Group Size: Any size group

Description: Each group of 10 - 15 people is instructed to organize a fashion show. The fashions the group creates use only newspaper and masking tape. They need to do the following:

1. Develop a theme for their show.

   Suggestions: *World leaders, the leaders' wedding, leaders from Disney World.*

2. Pick models, fashion designers and an M.C. for their show.

3. Design clothes

4. Develop a script to be read by the M.C.

5. Present the show to the other groups.

   Give the group five minutes to plan before they receive their material. Then give them 20 to 25 minutes to put it together. After that time, each group will present their show.

Learning Connection: Processing questions:

1. Did your group use their planning time wisely?

2. What organizational skills were needed to complete this project?

3. Were some people better suited to different tasks?

4. What is one thing you learned about organization?

Ownership

History: I first saw this activity at a leadership camp at which I was working. I have seen it done by a speaker named Phil Guliuza. Phil is from Louisiana. He is the state executive director of student councils and a well-known speaker/trainer.

Materials

1. A peanut for each person.
2. A brown paper lunch bag for every eight people

   Note: *Find out if anyone in the group has peanut allergies. If they do, make them observers or helpers for the activity.*

Time: 15 - 20 minutes

Group Size: Any number

Description: Have everyone in the group select a peanut. Explain that the peanut is their child. This is another simulation exercise. You need to get the group to buy into what you are trying to do. They need to give their child life. They will need to explain the basic facts about it. Examples would be:

1. Name   2. Age
3. Sex   4. Past times
5. Friends   6. Future plans

They need to think this out because, in the next step, they will give this information to another person. Have them pair up and give them a minute to tell their partner about their child. The partners' job is to listen as well as possible. Next, reverse the roles and have the other partner repeat the same activity.

After this sharing is finished, have the pairs find another pair and form a group of four. In this setting, each person takes a turn describing the partner's child (peanut). After each person shares, the owner of the peanut being described gets a chance to fill in any details that were left out. This is a good test of listening skills.

Lastly, the groups of four go together and form a group of eight. Supply each group of eight with a brown paper lunch bag. Tell them this a school bus picking up their children for school. Have all the group members put their peanuts in the bus and designate one of the group members as the driver. The drivers bring the buses to the front of the room and, under your direction, have them shake up the bags and make sudden moves with it. Tell them their children have a very bad bus driver. Tell them you heard of this problem and you have rushed to school to check on your children. Have the drivers return the bags to the group and dump out the peanuts. Instruct each participant to find their children.

Learning Connection: Processing questions:

1. How hard was it to create life for you child?
2. How could we have improved the listening process?
3. How did you feel when we put the peanuts in the bus?
4. Did you have any trouble finding your peanut?
5. How does this activity relate to listening?
6. How does this activity relate to ownership?
7. How would our total living environment improve if we cared about it as much as we cared about the peanut in this activity?

Shapes for Understanding

History: This is another example of an activity that allows people to look at themselves. I first saw this used by a student activity adviser from Pennsylvania. His name is Andy Costanza. He is a former National Student Council Adviser of the Year.

Materials: A copy of the Shapes for Understanding Worksheet for each participant, and an overhead or PowerPoint slide to show when you are doing the activity.

Time: 15 - 20 minutes

Group Size: Any number

Description: Pass out the shapes work sheet and have the group pick out their favorite shapes. I like to have them pick out three and rate them one through three. You could use any system that works for the objectives you are trying to emphasize. After the group has made their selections, go through the answers one by one. The answers are as follows:

1. EDUCATION
2. FOOD
3. POWER
4. SECURITY
5. MONEY
6. FAMILY
7. CREATIVITY
8. SEX (FRIENDSHIP)

As I reveal each shape, I take the time to discuss what they mean and why this category is important. Power, for example, is many times seen as a negative word. I point out we need people who want to assume power and take leadership positions. Number eight has two answers. If I am working with an adult group, I would use SEX. It gets a good laugh and can lead to a discussion about relationships. With student groups, I use FRIENDSHIP, which makes it appropriate.

Learning Connections: The point with any of these activities is to have the group understand in order to work effectively with others, we need to understand our own strengths and weaknesses. When we are able to do this, we also are able to look for strengths and weaknesses in others.

Shapes for Understanding
Worksheet

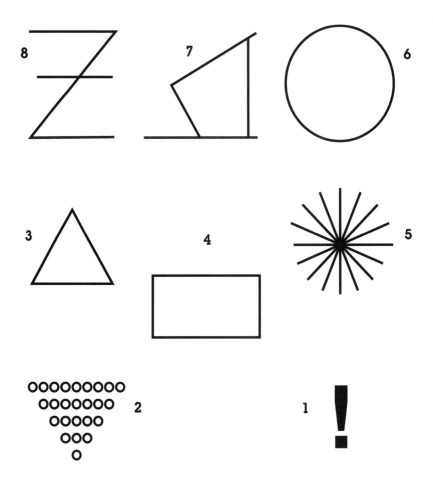

Carl Olson

Keys to Understanding

History: There is so much waste in our society. With a small amount of creativity, objects usually discarded can be useful tools for group or individual learning opportunities. I first saw this activity at a national workshop director's conference.

The presenter was giving my group many fantastic icebreaker ideas. A wealth of information was shared, but this particular activity made an impression on me. I have used it with many groups since with worthwhile results.

Materials: Each participant receives a computer key cap. All schools and computer outlets have old keyboards that have been discarded. You simply take a screwdriver or knife and pop off the keys you plan to use.

Time: 5-10 minutes

Group Size: Any number

Description: Pass around a container of computer keys and have each person select one key. Ask them to look at the key and decide how that key could represent them. Next, have

---

them pair up with another person and have them share the meaning of their key as it relates to them.

After the discussion period, have the participants form small groups or have one large group get together. Have the pairs introduce each other and report on what they shared. After each person tells what they've learned, allow the partners to fill in any information that might have been omitted. This allows each person in the group to be on stage and it shows how well they are listening to the explanations.

The computer keys can represent many areas in which information can be learned about people.

I like to keep notes or collect the data sheet and use the information for pop quizzes relating to the group, in later sessions.

Squat Game

History: This is another activity I have seen used in many places, but I cannot trace the origin. It is a simulation activity designed to show how living in poverty feels. Learning is always done best when the learner is activity involved. For safety reasons, and just plain practicality, we cannot take our students to countries where help is needed. Using video has some effect, but the basic understanding is difficult to get across, especially when we come from a society like  ours. This activity is unique in that it is simple, but it does get the point across.

Materials: The facilitator needs the directions and a copy of the story. The activity also requires helpers to select and tap people during the game. The number of helpers depends on the size of the group. This activity can be done with very large groups. I have done it with as many as 200 participants.

Description: The purpose of this activity is to give people a different perspective on hunger, helplessness, oppression and helping others.

The following steps should be taken to complete the activity:

1. Have the participants assume the squatting position. Knees bent like catcher sits in baseball, eyes shut.
2. They are not allowed to let their hands touch the ground.
3. They must remain in that squat position while the story is read.
4. If they are tapped on the shoulder, they may stand up, but must keep their eyes shut.
5. If they are touched a second time, they can open their eyes.

   The leader can do the tapping as they read, or designate helpers to tap people. For best results, about 25% of the participants should be tapped.

The Story

Try to empty your head. Forget about the test you had last hour, the paper due tomorrow, the chapters you have to read tonight. Forget about any problems that you might have carried with you into the room. For just a few moments, forget about all the millions of little things you have to do before you go to sleep tonight. Allow yourself to relax. Take a deep breath if you need to.

(Wait about a minute here.)

Now, try to think about something pleasant. Think about your education and the vast amount of possibilities you have of becoming a doctor, an engineer, a lawyer, a social worker or a teacher. What will you do when you leave school? What will life be like for you? Will you go to college? Will you have a big house or a small one? What kind of car will you drive? Will you make a lot of money, or will you work for minimum wage? Where will you be? What will you do?

Choices.... Decisions.... With whom will you spend your next vacation? With your friends? With your family? Think of your day so far. Think for just one minute about what you ate. Did you have breakfast? What did you have for lunch? For dinner? Did you get what your body needs? Did you get enough protein, carbohydrates and fat? If you chose, could you eat a well-balanced meal?

(Pause a moment or two, begin tapping people slowly.)

As most of you already know, there are famines all over the world. It has been going on for a long time. A huge number of people are literally starving to death—slowly, painfully, right now. They don't have many choices. They'll never go to college. They'll never face your decisions. If they die, even a choice for life is taken away. The quality of life is not even an issue when you are trying to survive merely until tomorrow; one more day, still hoping that help will come. Although they may not know it, they share their pain with millions of sisters and brothers all over the world. They feel isolated and alone in their pain. These people could be in Guatemala, Nicaragua or El Salvador. There also are the suffering and degraded people in Mexico and the Philippines, along with the migrant farm workers and the inner city poor in the United States. In fact, they share their poverty and destitution with people in every country on the face of this small planet. AND IT DOESN'T GO AWAY....

It hurts in the very center of their being. It hurts mentally and physically. They feel it in their legs when they cramp up, because they do not get enough of the right food, and it is painful. They wonder if it will ever end. Sometimes, they see people who have no pain. They see people who stand free and strong, but who are completely blind to what is happening around them. The free and the strong often do not see the suffering and the pain of those around them. They are ignorant to what is happening around them. These people are blind but others that do suffer - see. Those people continue to wonder if the pain will ever stop; if this life will ever end.

Some of you have already been touched. You have experienced the presence of a hand that has eliminated your pain. Some of you have been touched twice. You are not only out of pain, but you are fully awake with your eyes open. You see, without question, those who are in pain. You begin to slowly realize how important a single touch can be. You realize the power that a single touch can have. With a single touch, you can relieve the pain of one who suffers and open up the eyes of one who is blind. You realize the freedom you have to move and to choose. You are free to touch someone. We are all free to touch the hungry people of the world and bring them from darkness into light.

Discussion Questions:

1. How did it feel to squat?
2. How did you feel when you were tapped?
3. How did react to this game?
4. When did you stop focusing on the story and concentrate on your own pain?
5. What was going through your mind when your eyes were closed and I was talking about blindness?
6. Did anyone kneeling have the urge to stand up? To sit down? To open your eyes?
   - Did anyone stand up, sit down, or open your eyes who wasn't touched?
   - What could be the symbolic meaning of breaking these rules? Do hungry people have this option?
8. Did you feel mad or angry after this game? How did it affect you?
9. What role did the person who tapped people play? Who actually touches the hungry people of the world? What do you think each group symbolizes? (i.e., standing with eyes closed, standing with eyes open, squatting with eyes closed, or eyes open and touching people)
10. Where do you think you are in one of the groups? (Indicate answer by raising hands.)

Who Has the Power

Materials: The following will be needed:

1. Dice—You will need one die for each small group in which you are working.

2. A bag of candy—Choose a type that the participants will recognize and something they will like.

Description: This version of the dice game is designed to teach the concept that we do not always get what we want. The person who shared it with me used it while working with students in a divorce group. The game starts with the participants sitting in a circle with a bowl of candy in the center of the group. There should be less pieces of candy than there are people in the group. The participants take turns shaking the die. They are trying to shake a six. If they shake a six, they are allowed to take a piece of candy.

When all of the candy is gone, the game continues. When a six comes up after the candy is gone, the participant who shakes a six is allowed to take a piece of candy from any of the group members. Play is continued for a predetermined time.

Part 4
Special Activities

The activities in this section contain group projects that are better suited to all school, or large group meetings. They take place over a longer period of time. They are designed to build spirit, appreciation and awareness.

A Day In the Life
Photo Contest

History: I got the idea for this activity from a fellow student council adviser. We used it in my school for several years. It is a way to get students involved, and it provides an outlet for students with creative interests.

Materials: See the list of directions for the necessary materials

Time: Two days for photography, one week to complete the projects.

Group Size: Any number

Directions:

1. Students are allowed to bring cameras to school for two consecutive days.

2. They may take pictures only with permission, and they are not allowed to disturb classes.

3. On Friday of the designated week, the students who choose to enter the contest are given a plain sheet of poster paper.

4. They use the pictures they took and their imaginations to make posters about what a day at school is like for them.

5. They are instructed to put their names on the back of their completed projects.

6. All posters are displayed in the cafeteria and numbered.

7. We asked the staff to judge the posters and rate the top five.

8. A committee of student council members took the top five posters to each fifth grade classroom. Our school was a 6 to 8 middle school, so this contact with grade five students was part of the orientation process. We had the grade five students vote to help decide the top five place winners.

9. We gave $50 to first place, $40 to second, $30 to third, $20 to fourth and $10 to fifth. All students who entered posters were invited to a pizza party, where we had a drawing for five additional prizes of five dollars each.

We always held this contest during the fall of the year, and we have it culminate near the end of first quarter. The posters were on display during parent/teacher conferences. The parents enjoyed looking at them, and it was a great PR tool.

Family Numbers

History: To truly know someone, we have to go beyond basic introductions. This exercise uses basic algebra to find out personal information at a deeper level. I used it when I was working with groups and I kept the results in order to help me with insight on the individuals in the group.

Materials: Each group member will need paper and something with which to write. You can have a "Family Size" worksheet for each person, or make an overhead and project the worksheet. The "Family Size" worksheet is shown in figure #1.

Time: 10 - 20 minutes

Group Size: Any size group

Description: Have the individual or group do the math problem you see in figure #1. It works best if you talk them through it, having them put in their own personal information.

They will end up with either a one, two or three digit number. The number they come up with represents information about their families.

Example— 121

A person with this final number would have 1 brother, 2 sisters and 1 living grandparent.

Units Place = Living Grandparents

Tens Place = Sisters

Hundreds Place = Brothers

(Note: If the person has a 2 digit number, it means there are no brothers.)

Learning Connections: I like to use this activity to teach the need to go beyond the obvious when getting to know people. It works as a conversation starter. I always save the final results if I am going to have prolonged contact with the group. As a teacher or coach, I would keep the number handy as a reference about the individual person.

Figure # 1
Family Size Worksheet

_____ = Number of Brothers

X 2

_____ =

+ 3

_____ =

X 5

_____ =

_____ + Number of Sisters

_____ =

X 10

_____ =

_____ + Number of Living Grandparents

_____ =

- 150

_____ = Special Number

Random Acts of Kindness

History: I first heard about this activity from a fellow student council adviser from Oklahoma. His name is Gary Oberste. He is a great resource with many innovative and practical ideas. His contact information can be found in the resources section.

Materials: This is an appreciation activity in which you will need one set of these materials for each person you plan to honor. The set of materials are as follows:

1. A decorative basket or container.
2. One helium, "Thank You" balloon.
3. Ten assorted candy bars.
4. Ten blank thank you notes.

Time: 10 - 20 minutes

Group Size: Any number

Description: Psychologists say appreciation is one of the four things all people want in order to be fulfilled. This activity sets up a situation where people take the time to practice appreciation. More importantly, the people involved will be modeling this desired behavior for others to see. The following are the rules we used in our school setting:

1. Every quarter we chose one student council member from each grade to represent us.
2. We bought three decorative helium balloons that said "Thank You" on them.
3. The balloons were weighted and attached to a string, along with a pack of thank you cards.
4. At a faculty meeting, the three chosen students presented the balloons to the teachers of their choice. We asked them to make brief statements as to why they chose to honor the teachers they did.
5. After the meeting, each of the honored teachers were instructed to write appreciation notes and have the students pass their balloons and extra thank you cards on to other staff members.
6. We asked that the balloons be passed once per day from staff member to staff member. After a week, the balloons were collected and the process was over.

We found that a great deal of good will was established in the original presentation. That same good will was then spread throughout the school in the ensuing days. At the same time, the students in our school were seeing appreciation behavior modeled by the staff. We used three balloons because it fit well with the size of our staff. For larger organizations, I would suggest adjusting the number of balloons as needed.

Leaving Your Mark

HISTORY: This is another activity that I learned from Steve Spangler of *Steve Spangler Science*. In the activity, participants share a personal symbol on t-shirts using permanent markers and alcohol. The results are special because the alcohol makes a tie died effect and the group members are able to take a little piece of everyone home.

MATERIALS: You need the following:

1. A set of colored Sharpie® permanent fine point markers. The best colors are red, green and blue. You should have enough markers so that everyone has a choice of the colors they want to use.

2. A plastic cup for each participant.

3. A rubber band for each participant.

4. Small spray bottles or small glue bottles filled with alcohol.

Carl Olson

DESCRIPTION: In this activity, each participant is asked to come up with a symbol. It should be designed to represent something special about them. The symbol should fit in an area the size of the mouth of the cup. Have all the participants start by putting their own symbol on their personal shirt.

The symbol is applied by first choosing an area of the shirt. Next, they stretch that area over the cup, secure it with a rubber band, and draw the symbol in the area created. After the drawing is finished, the alcohol is applied. Adults or group leaders should be in charge of the alcohol. The application of the alcohol will make the colors in the drawing run.

The activity is continued by having the participants circulate around the room sharing their symbols with each other. This is best used as a culminating activity. Allow for thirty to forty-five minutes judging the time by the size of the group. Play soft relaxing music during the symbol sharing time. The symbols can be made permanent by heat setting the shirts in a dryer for ten minutes.

Resources

Boyte, P., Jacobson, M., & Jones R. (1977). *Focus.* Meadow Vista, CA: Learning for Living.

Bowman, R. (2002). *50 Magic tricks using common objects.* Chapin, SC: Youth Light.

Bowman, R. (2003). *201 mind bogglers,* Chapin, SC: Youth Light.

Bowman, R. (2004). *The magic counselor.* Chapin, SC: Youth Light.

Butler, S., & Rohnke, K. (1995). *Quicksilver.* Dubuque, IA: Kendall/Hunt Publishing.

Cain, J., & Jolliff, B. (1998). *Teamwork & teamplay.* Dubuque, IA: Kendall/Hunt Publishing.

Fleugelman, A. (ed.) (1978). *The new games book.* Tiburon, CA: Headlands Press.

Fleugelman, A. (ed.) (1981). *More new games!* Tiburon, CA: Headlands Press.

Foster, E. (1989). *Energizers and icebreakers for all ages and stages.* Minneapolis, MN: Educational Media Corporation.

Foster-Harrison, E. (1994). *More energizers and icebreakers for all ages and stages, book II.* Minneapolis, MN: Educational Media Corporation.

Harris, F. (1962). *Great games to play with groups.* Torrance, CA: Frank Schaffer Publishing.

Hazouri, S.P., & McLaughlin, M.S. (1993). *Warm ups & wind downs: 101 activities for moving and motivating groups.* Minneapolis, MN: Educational Media Corporation.

Irvin, J. (1997). *Chicken poop in my bowl.* Tulsa, OK: J&C Publishing

Jackson, T. (1993). *Activities that teach.* Cedar City, UT: Red Rock Publishing.

Jackson, T. (1995) *More activities that teach.* Cedar City, UT: Red Rock Publishing.

Jackson, T. (2000). *Still more activities that teach.* Cedar City, UT: Red Rock Publishing.

McBride, W. (1997). *Entertaining an elephant.* San Francisco, CA: First Pearl Street Press.

Rohnke, K. (1991). *The bottomless bag.* Dubuque, IA: Kendall/Hunt Publishing.

Rohnke, K. (1989). *Cowtails and cobras II*. Dubuque, IA: Kendall/Hunt Publishing.

Rohnke, K. (1984). *Silver bullets*. Dubuque, IA, Kendall/Hunt Publishing.

Rose, E. (1997). *Presenting and training with magic*. New York, NY: McGraw-Hill Publishing.

Weinstein, M., & Goodman J. (1980). *Playfair*. San Luis Obispo, CA: Impact Publishers.

Wenc, C.C. (1993). *Cooperation: Learning through laughter*. Minneapolis, MN: Educational Media Corporation.

Organizations / Vendors

Many of the magical props needed for the activities in this book are included in the **Impact Pak** available from **www.educationalmedia.com** or **www.energizerolson.com**. Check Energizer Olson or the magic vendors listed below for other props.

A.B.E.E.: *Ropes course construction and training* www.abbeeinc.com

Daytona Magic: *magic distributor* www.daytonamagic.com

Difference Makers: *speakers, publications & information* www.differencemakers.com

Educational Media: *publisher* www.educationalmedia.com

Learning for Living: *training programs, educational materials* www.learningforliving.com

Hank Lee's Magic Factory: *magic distributor* www.magicfac.com

International Brotherhood of Magicians: *National Organization* www.magician.org

National Association of School Councils: *training programs, conference, resources* www.nasc.org

Oriental Trading: *inexpensive materials* www.orientaltrading.com

Project Adventure: *training programs, educational materials, publications* www.pa.org

U.S. Toy: *inexpensive materials* www.ustoy.com

Steve Spangler Science: *educational materials, speaking & training* www.stevespanglerscience.com

The Brain Store: *workshops, conferences, publisher* www.brainstore.com

Twin Cities Magic & Costume: *magic distributor* www.twincitiesmagic.com

Speakers / Trainers

Anderson, L.: *Trainer, executive director of the North Dakota Association of School Councils* Les.Anderson@sendit.nodak.edu

Boyte, P.: *Author, publisher, motivational speaker and owner of Learning for Living Inc.* www.learningfor living.com

Cochran, C.: *Executive director of the North Carolina Association of School Councils* colby@ctc.net

Collar, B.: *Motivational Speaker and Trainer* pma@billcollar.com

Fiscus, L.: *Editor of the Leadership for Student Activities Magazine* leadershipmag@principal.org

Gugliuzza, P.: *Motivational speaker and Executive Director of the Louisiana Association of School Councils* PGugli2271@aol.com

Jensen, E.: *Author, trainer, speaker and owner of The Brain Store* www.brainstore.com

Miley, C.: *Speaker, adviser and M.S. Executive Director for the Ohio Association of School Councils* Cmiley@webtv.net

Olson, P.: *Student activities director for Minneapolis Public Schools* Pam.Olson@mpls.k12.mn.us

Postelwaite, A.: *Speaker, trainer and executive director of the Minnesota Association of School Councils* ann@mail.massp.org

Peak, R.: *Speaker, magician, hypnotist* www.russpeak.com

Riedel, P.: *Adviser, student activities director, speaker, trainer* phupfer@piuxi.org

Reuhm, E.: *Speaker, trainer, author* reumer@estreet.com

Smith, S.P.: *Magician, publisher, distributor of magic tricks* www.spsmagic.com

Saunders, S.: *Speaker, trainer., author, leadership camp director* ssaunders@leadershipinovations.com

Smith, M.: *Speaker, author, trainer, and owner of Difference Makers* www.differencemakers.com

Spangler, S.: *Speaker, trainer, magician, and owner of Steve Spangler Science* www.stevespanglerscience.com

Stevenson, A.: *Speaker, trainer, U. of Minnesota extension educator* Steve020@umn.edu